HIGH ON SOU!

TELL ME IT'S JUST A RUMOR BERRY

Al Abrams

NEW HAVEN PUBLISHING

Published 2025
First Edition
www.newhavenpublishingltd.com
newhavenpublishing@gmail.com

All Rights Reserved
The rights of Al Abrams as the author of this work, have been asserted in accordance with the Copyrights, Designs and Patents Act 1988.
No part of this book may be re-printed or reproduced or utilized in any form or by any electronic, mechanical or other means, now unknown or hereafter invented, including photocopying, and recording, or in any information storage or retrieval system, without the written permission of the
Authors and Publisher.

Cover © Pete Cunliffe
pcunliffe@blueyonder.co.uk

Copyright © 2025 Al Abrams
All rights reserved
ISBN: 978-1-915975-21-8

Billy Johnsen, Al Abrams, Johnny (JJ) Jones, Berry Gordy, Jr, Jackie Wilson, Robert Bateman

The Berry Gordy/Motown family (the terms are interchangeable) in happier days as they depart Detroit's Metro Airport for London, 1964. From left to right: The then-married Harvey Fuqua and Gwen Gordy Fuqua; the also then-married Anna Gordy Gaye and Marvin Gaye; Mrs. Berry Gordy, Sr., and another Gordy sister and Motown executive, Loucye Gordy Wakefield.

Forewords

Al Abrams was a music press guy on an early Motown mission to make sure that all of us artists at Motown were recognized and celebrated for the music we gave to and performed for the world!

He deserves a Star for doing what most press men walk away from doing. He promoted the artists and their music while staying behind the stage curtains.

Al was a hell of a media man.

Thanks Buddy!
Otis Williams, The Temptations

Al Abrams was a very dear friend of mine.

Al was Motown's incredible press officer. He created the hype and the romance between Motown Music and the world. Al cared about every artist that was on the Motown Record Label.

He is the one that dreamt up the two famous slogans that Motown still uses, "The Detroit Sound" and "Motown: The Sound of Young America."

Al broke down the black and white music barriers that separated dance floors.

And, it is because of Al that we, the Supremes, were featured on major magazine covers, newspapers and television.

Thank you Al, my dear friend, for all that you did in those days of civil rights and war unrest to make Motown a global Record Hit. You made us a hit!
Love – Your Friend, Mary Wilson

Being one of the pioneers of the Motown Sound in 1962, I got to know Al Abrams personally and he became a good and supportive friend.

Al was the DJs best friend in those early days. He would walk into the record places where they would have a white artist list and a black artist list. Al chose the BLACK list.

Al broke down the color barriers dividing our music. I don't know if he ever used a gun or not. But, he got all the jocks to play our music and we love him for that.

Motown would not have been famous had not Al Abrams went and knocked those doors down

Al Abrams ... was the best Motown press guy ever.

Al as the DJs best friend would go to their radio stations. They all got to know him and love his press style.

However, radio station program directors would tell their DJS not to play any Motown Sound.

Al broke those walls and knocked those music doors down. I love AL!

I was glad when they asked me to cut the ribbon when his Motown Black and White Exhibit opened in Saginaw Michigan at the Castle Museum after his death. Al's exhibit was embraced with total Music Love.

I believe that every fan of music who loves Motown will embrace and love the story of Al Abrams, Motown's phenomenal Press Officer.

Al had to know everything about Motown from its inside to its outside.

Al's Motown Black & White Exhibit rivals Motown's Historical Museum, Hitsville, from a very different and unique historical perspective.

Al Abrams, Motown's young Press Officer was the background of "The Motown Sound." "Motown: The Sound of Young America."

Martha Reeves, Martha & The Vandellas

Let me say something about, Al Abrams. A lot of people didn't know AL ABRAMS and who he is or what he did for Motown. Well, let me tell you ... He is one of the true hidden behind the scene Motown stars.

I believe he was the first person that Berry hired at eighteen years old. He was energetic, a visionary and had all the energy and bright ideas as Berry did.

Berry was very good at picking artists. When he picked Al Abrams, Gordy selected a true artist. Al became the publicist for Motown Records.

He did so many wonderful things that I can't really spell out in a few stage minutes all that he did.

But, people should know and read the Motown plus history of Al Abrams.

Al was the first hire of berry Gordy to work at Tamla/Motown Records. Al is the one who came up with the slogan, "Motown: The Sound of Young America." Now, if that's NOT BIG, I'll kiss your ass.

This is one of the things. He is the one that got the Supremes on the cover of major magazines and world newspapers.

He helped make Motown to become exactly what it is today.

If it wasn't for Al , I don't think I'd be here, nor would a lot of the other artists. He was the Motown Star that didn't get a chance to shine. So, we are going to shine for him tonight. A Detroit Music prestigious award for a wonderful, wonderful guy. Al was our Motown World MUSIC Media Hero."

Duke Fakir, Four Tops

I am from Detroit, and very proud to be, as all Detroiters are. There is something 'in the air' for sure. The city is irrepressible, brave, warm, friendly, energetic, clever, and very very human. I was asked to write a foreword for Al's book, and I guess , unwittingly I just described him. We met when I was doing one of my documentaries for my long running stint on bbc radio 2, and a bond was forged. We became friends. Al was one of a kind. His stories and memories are legendary. I could have sat and listened to him forever. I was weaned on Motown. I loved Motown and I still know all the Temptations dance steps!

Al and I connected easily on every level. I miss him and his shining light.

This book is important to anyone and everyone who ever bought a Motown single. And I think I can safely say that includes most people.

Al was there ... Al knows the story… and most important ... AL IS HONEST about the music history and the artists he represented. R.I.P. my Detroit brother your story lives on.

Suzi Quatro xx

The story gets curiouser and curiouser, but that's not surprising since we are dealing with the unclassifiable Alan a great personal friend. We had a number of interesting Music escapades from James Brown and the Rolling Stones to his immersion into Motown Records and Stax-Volt.

Al was the epitome of a press guy obsessed with focusing upon the record labels and artists that he had to get the media spotlight to focus upon. It was not an easy job for Al to get done, especially with Civil Rights and the Vietnam War raging.

All obsessed music fans should look forward to further revelations in this book.

It is honest music history from a guy who had to deal with all the sordid details of the music industry as was required of him. All I can say is "CHEERS!" to a talented music guy who breathed and lived the record labels and artists he represented by using his media savvy talent to sell the world their music.

Al was a good friend and an interesting press guy!

David Dalton
(Dalton was the author of some fifteen books, 7 of them New York Times bestsellers. He was a founding editor of Rolling Stone Magazine, writing many of the magazine's early cover stories.)

My dear Al Abrams was one of a kind, both as an innovative force in the music business and as a publicist who was responsible for putting a fledgling Motown and its artists well and truly on the media map. He always had an eye for a story. What a talent! His reputation in, and knowledge of, the music business earned him the up-most respect and that was no mean feat in the competitive world of the printed word. On a personal platform, Al was the man I regularly turned to for help and anecdotes with my Motown projects: Al's advice and guidance was freely given, while his tales were priceless.

Without Al being the pivotal force in the media world, many artists would have floundered for headline news columns without him. And it was his wry sense of humour, honesty, dedication and occasional 'poetic licence' that earned him the title of Legendary Press Officer, some of which we were invited to share in his first book Hype & Sou!

This new book, promising more of the same with added adventures and insights, will be a must for every music industry connoisseur. Thank you Al for everything! The media misses you and so do I.

Sharon Davis
Co-Author of Motown To Londontown: Hitsville UK published 2021

Al was more than just a friend to me; he was a guiding force during the early planning stages of the National Rhythm & Blues Hall of Fame.

Al spent countless hours on the phone with me, sharing stories about the legends of Motown and other greats like my hero, James Brown, whom he had worked with.

Al's deep connection to the history of R&B music, which he had helped shape since 1959, was invaluable. He believed in my vision and wanted to see the National Rhythm & Blues Hall of Fame, come to life to preserve the legacy of the genre he loved so much.

Al's generosity extended beyond words. He sent me memorabilia, anticipating the day the this one-of-kind Hall of Fame would open. Among the treasures he shared were photographs he had taken of R&B icons, and perhaps most notably, an autographed pocketbook from Mary Wilson of the Supremes. These gifts were a testament to his belief in the project and his desire to see the history of R&B honored.

In 2016, it was a special moment for me to be able to induct Al into the National Rhythm & Blues Hall of Fame. It was a fitting tribute to a man who had given so much to the music industry and to me personally. Al's hard work and contributions helped to shape the R&B landscape, and his memory continues to inspire me in the ongoing mission to preserve and celebrate the history of Rhythm & Blues. I miss Al dearly, but his legacy lives on in the Hall of Fame and in the stories and artifacts he so graciously shared.

LaMont "ShowBoat" Robinson
Founder | CEO
National Rhythm & Blues HOF Foundation

I had the pleasure of meeting Al Abrams while collaborating on a project involving an artist I represented.

Our partnership continued at Plateau Music, where we handled national public relations for the label.

Our professional relationship evolved into a meaningful friendship over time, and I miss our in-depth discussions about music that transcended everyday conversations.

Al will be deeply missed, and his contributions to the music industry will not be forgotten.

Tony Mantor
Plateau Music
Tony Mantor's: Almost Live… Nashville Podcast
Nashville, TN

Al Abrams was inducted as an honorary member of the Michigan Rock and Roll Legends Hall of Fame in 2011. Honorary Inductions were established to recognize individuals behind-the-scenes who were significant contributors to the history of Michigan rock and roll.

Al worked as the national promotion director for Tamla Records and Jobete Music, and later as the director of advertising and public relations for Motown. His memorable phrase, "The Sound of Young

America," and his other groundbreaking promotional ideas were instrumental in helping the company become one of the most successful record labels in the history of popular music.

Gary J. Johnson - Michigan Rock and Roll Legends Hall of Fame

Most of us have a moment when, not necessarily with our knowledge at the time, the life we are leading or planning is put into high gear and jettisons us into a new path. It may be a path we crave or one we hadn't even thought of yet.

My jet powered moment was delivered to me by a man I hadn't met yet… Al Abrams. Unbeknownst to me Al had recommended me for a job at the fifth largest morning newspaper in North America (I'm told), The Detroit Free Press. From that point on Stage 2 of my professional life began.

Here was a man who saw some talent in a young Canadian writer with only local exposure in his hometown and brought it to a vast and impressive audience. Al knew how to do that for people, and willingly and lovingly did so.

As they say Al was Motown before it even had a name. As a PR man his intelligence and style brought that "magic moment" to artists ranging from The Supremes to James Brown and special labels beyond Motown including the legendary Stax Records and Invictus. And he NEVER got enough credit for his brilliant work.

Thanks Al.

Yes, thanks Al for taking a guy barely out of his teens to center stage in journalism and the music world.

Mike Gormley
L.A. Personal Development
lapersdev.com

Even if someone was to claim that "The Sound of Young America" is no longer young, they could not deny that it has aged like a fine wine. "The Motown Sound" has proven time and time again to be truly timeless, whether manifesting itself in the 90s with the resurgence of vocal groups and boy bands, the booming industry of sampling in the mainstream music of the 2000s, the throwback sounds of 2010s artists like Bruno Mars, Meghan Trainor, Robin Thicke, Aloe Blacc, Mayer Hawthorne, and Leon Bridges, or the label's 60th anniversary that will help ring in the 2020s. Motown's music is timeless, and helped set the template for countless iconic composers and performers who were either on the label or following in its footsteps. Motown helped break barriers by introducing African American artists to listeners across America and across the world. However, those listeners may never have heard those barrier breaking voices without the work of Al Abrams, Motown's press director.

Al's tireless dedication and strategy helped Motown climb the charts and become the iconic label that the entire world knows and loves. For those stories, you should check out his books! However, I can absolutely speak to his character and to his love and devotion to the Motown story. Al Abrams cared deeply about the Motown artists, musicians, songwriters, producers, and behind-the-scenes team members who made "what's in the grooves" count so much.

I met Al Abrams electronically at first. It was February of 2013, and the Funk Brothers were set to receive a star on the Hollywood Walk of Fame. I was assisting Funks' guitarist Eddie Willis with getting to California from Mississippi, as he was having travel difficulties stemming from a long struggle with polio. Al and I connected over Motown, and his enthusiasm to see a younger generation embracing the music he worked so hard to push. He told me stories of his own daughter opening for The Contours, singing a Martha Reeves song onstage, and seeing her embrace an older generation's art. As a fledgling professional musician, songwriter, producer, and performer in my own right, he gave me some wonderful advice even though he barely knew me - Al told me that "You must always look at everything from an unbiased perspective. We are in a music industry where fact and fiction need to be reviewed and analyzed before we say 'yes'."

Through the years, as I continued to keep in contact with Mr. Abrams and learn more about his work, I realized how much he lived those words. Al Abrams was truly unbiased.

Berry Gordy founded his record company and hired Al Abrams in the same year, 1959.

In a time when segregation was still legal in the United States, Al was not afraid to be a White employee of an African American employer, he was not afraid of promoting African American artists to a divided world, and he was not afraid of championing the music and musicians that he believed in. Every time I had the pleasure of corresponding with Mr. Abrams, he insisted that I "just call him Al." However, it never felt right to me - as a professional in the music industry, I would not have my career without Motown.

My early mentors included members of The Funk Brothers. My first professional touring gig was with the Four Tops & Temptations. My first album featured performances by some of my own Motown heroes. I may have never known these people who truly shaped and changed my life without the tireless work of Al Abrams, and I felt that he had earned all the respect I could possibly offer. It became a bit of a running joke between us. He'd tell me that "as Paul Simon would say, 'you can call me Al.'"

The last time I got to see him in person was at an event in Detroit that was celebrating Motown: The Musical opening at the Fisher Theater. Just as always, he was humble, kind, welcoming, and overflowing with valuable advice.

It was wonderful seeing him happily on stage with Berry, Smokey, Stevie, and so many Motown family members singing the Motown Company Song.

I am honored to have counted him as a friend, and will forever be thankful for the work he did - not only for Motown, Stax, Holland-Dozier-Holland's Invictus/Hot Wax, and more, but for helping to lead the way and forge a path ahead for countless younger artists, songwriters, performers, and professionals to follow themselves. "The Sound of Young America" lives on.

Drew Schultz, Motown Band Drummer, Songwriter, Teacher

Al Abrams just appeared one day in the Windsor Star newsroom in the mid 1980s. I wasn't sure what to make of this guy from Detroit, who was sitting at the desk next to me.

He turned out to be a welcomed newsroom character who would regale us with tales about his days as Motown's press officer. I would sit there like a little kid with rapt attention.

There were doubters – even me to an extent – about the validity of his music stories.

These questions persisted until the day Al and then Windsor Star photographer Randall Moore crossed over to Detroit to cover the official opening of the Motown Museum.

"I thought this would hold Al's feet to the flame with regard to the truth. When we got to Hitsville USA ... we got to about an arm's length away from Smokey Robinson. He looked at me and smiled, said hello, then looked at Al. "Hi Smoke", Al said. Smokey took a half-beat for memory to kick in, then, with a broad smile said: "Al! How are you doing! Great to see you again!" Moore recalls. "And that was that."

Al settled into the newsroom and never shied away from the daily assignments. He made friends easily and was always in touch with local and international events, especially what was making the news across the river in Detroit. Al was a news junky.

He confided in me one day that he hoped to get an invitation to George Bush's presidential inauguration. "Sure, Al, how the hell are you going to swing that," I said.

Well, I'll be darned if he didn't, always the PR man. (Music relevant integrated story too.)

It didn't take long to discover that Al was a tad paranoid. I once left a note in his desk saying that I had gone through all of his stuff – of course, I didn't – and he was thrown off his game for the rest of the day. We laughed at his expense.

So, what was it that Al brought to the Windsor Star?

"I was impressed by his Jimmy Breslin attitude towards the world," said Mike Dunnell, who was assistant managing editor at the time, referring to the legendary columnist for the New York Daily News. Dunnell said Al was a character at a time when there were few in the newsroom.

But as quickly as he arrived, Al was gone. Al did occasionally call me for several years after that to talk about his latest adventure.

And I would listen with interest because Al could always tell a great story.

Richard J. Brennan, Retired Toronto Star political reporter

Say it LOUD. Al Abrams said it vociferously from the second he joined Motown.

He was the label's first Soul messenger and as the tiny fledgling Detroit company turned into the massive Hitsville juggernaut. He made it his hyper holy mission to spread the word .

Not just LOUD but very PROUD. That pride in "the sound of young America" resonated in every page Al sent me when we were working on his previous book "Hype & Soul!" which delved into his publicity feats that helped make Berry Gordy's empire so incredibly successful. The book demonstrated Al's love for the young genius singers, songwriters, producers and arrangers who created the music which conquered the World. Of course it did. But it also shone a light on the many people in the background who were also an integral part in creating magic on West Grand Boulevard. It was the little people who made something big.

I was fascinated by those pages from Al. As soon as I had devoured one chapter (I was supposed to edit them but Al's prose did not invite such brutality.) I was desperate to receive the next. It's been a long wait but "High On Soul: Tell Me It's Just A Rumor Berry" means I will finally have more pages from Al to eagerly consume.

Sadly he is not here to send them to me but his words live on - LOUD and PROUD.

Neil Rushton – Music UK

My cousin Al… I remember growing up and knowing that my Cousin Al was famous! I had always heard that he was "responsible for Motown"! Well, for Berry Gordy and many black artists, maybe he was? He helped many to be seen and heard and cross that racial divide that helped to change music for all time!

You would never know that to meet him. He was an unassuming kind gentle man with a great personality and an interest in people.

We met for the first time in 2009 in Berlin, Germany where he was doing a show he created along with Mickey Stevenson and produced by Bernhard Kurz called "Memories of Motown". They had a successful month run starring Martha Reeves, The Contours and The Miracles, as well as Bobby Wilson, Roz Thomas and Denita Asberry.

The show told the story of Motown with narration and music, celebrating the 50th Anniversary of Motown.

It was my Mom who connected Bernhard with Al. She was very good at bringing artists, producers, agents and talent together with her company, "The Entertainment Network". She was a very special woman, Al told me he always wanted to write a book about her.

His Motown show was coming to an end and our show, "Stars in Concert" was going into The Estrel Hotel and Convention Center…so it felt like, the ships that would've passed in the night got to have a few overlapping days together! We talked and laughed for hours!

We felt connected immediately! He was special like that. We stayed close by phone and e-mail. He was writing a book about Bobby Wilson…and we talked about my Mom. He was always working on something and thinking about what he wanted to do next. He was curious and he cared about people and what they we're going through. I loved that about him.

Sherie Ray Parker, Singer

Dedication by Al Abrams before his passing

My impending death is difficult for me. I have only a few moments in earthly time left in my life. How do I compensate to those I ever wronged and to those I deeply love?

My tears are an endless stream. Reliving life's memories knowing that I will soon become a memory only makes my heart bleed. I'm leaving behind my loved ones, memories, memoirs, possessions and lyrics that I wrote reflective of our world and humanity as I have seen it and see it as it will play in the future.

As the world spins its diverse records, may the music unite and not divide people. I have titled it, "The Glass Gladiator".

I'm praying that G-D will meet me at His Coliseum and allow me entrance into His Kingdom.

Life plays never-ending songs of who we are from birth to death. My last song is on the turntable.

This book and all that I have written, recorded or am leaving behind is dedicated to my beautiful wife, Nancy Cecilia, and my beautiful granddaughters, Margot Emery Reiter and Luca Eliannah Cecilia Hutka.

May G-D watch over my family and bless them. I LOVE YOU NOW & FOREVER … Let our MUSIC Play.

Your HUSBAND & GRANDFATHER AL

* I, also, dedicate my book to those Heroes and Heroines that have and will follow.

GLOBAL MUSIC FOR PEACE IN THE UNIVERSE.

Music plays in world coliseums with a multifaceted surround sound that streams

G-D'S hope for us.

Nancy Abrams

Margot and Paul Reiser Jr at Detroit Historical Museum

Luca with Martha Reeves at her birthday party

Content

Forewords   5

Dedication   17

1 Glass Gladiator   23

2 Motown Man of Valor - Your Brother in Arms   47

3 Stolen Valor – D-Day Torpedo - Bury the Manuscript   71

4 Unpublished Motown Memoirs 1968/1969 &
     Abrams Interview   79

5 Script for a Record Label Television Series   118

6 Why Motown Black & White?   142

7 The Final Turntable Spin   155

1

Glass Gladiator

AL ABRAMS, Motown's Press Officer's Final Press Release

Motown's Press Officer Pens Farewell Lyrics to Inspire and Celebrate Ordinary Global Humanity Heroes!

Prior to his death, Al wrote what he referred to as his final "*Press Release*" in the form of lyrics. He entitled it, Glass Gladiator.

Being the Press Officer for Motown, *Al Abrams*, was always behind the concert stage doors. But, a press officer is multi-faceted and multi-talented.

Al co-wrote a song, *"I Love the Way You Love"*, with Berry Gordy, Motown's Founder, while riding in a car. Marv Johnson was the Motown Artist who recorded it.

After learning of his impending death, Al took the advice given to him by Leonard Cohen – 'Write final and meaningful lyrics about your view of life with a heartfelt message. Give them to someone you trust. Tell them to follow through for you.'

In the final days of his life in 2015, Al penned his lyrics. It is his final press release and a farewell to life. His lyrics are timeless and powerful. His words reflect the choice ordinary people *must* choose to protect Family, Flag and Humanity at great personal loss.

Al's last request to have his lyrics set to a musical score is being undertaken by two incredible and talented Motown heroes and composers. Al wanted his song to meld his hometown of Detroit, MI USA and his Motown roots with Israel and his Jewish culture to reach across all Global Borders and reverberate under all Free World Flags and their people.

Humanity is on the Firing Line. Al's lyrics and the artistry of the music composition and vocals will tell the story of courage under fire. We are all fragile Glass Gladiators. Survival of HUMANITY will become the legacy for the future of all global children.

Motown's Drew Schultz and Paul Riser, Sr. have offered their unconditional help to complete Al's last request. Revising his original lyrics so they can be set to a musical score is what they have undertaken. The University of Michigan, Music Department, is taking Al's revised lyrics and setting it to a musical score.

With all that is going on in the world, I find that Al's own press officer /journalism/writer storyline and the *Glass Gladiator* lyrics that he wrote, prior to his impending death, are very attune to and in touch with the reality of war and loss.

The timing for his lyrics is in sync with the global unrest and the atrocities unfolding. It tells a human story. And that story is relevant to every battle fought by a gladiator. Many gladiators never return.

Life has not been easy for any of us as we lived through a Covid pandemic and lockdown and now are thrust into a world where war and terrorists infiltrate our daily lives. Other, relevant world factors are, also, creating a world on the edge.

Life is a series of intense battles. And, becoming a glass gladiator who never cracks is challenging. Al's lyrics tell the story as to the fragility of a gladiator's sword on a battlefield.

Al wanted his lyrics set to music to coincide with an unfolding story relevant to a noble global cause. Al always looked at history and how it is repetitive and, oftentimes, revised by unscrupulous people and entities. Al believed that we learn from factual history and not from revisionists rewriting history.

You either survive by becoming a glass gladiator that fights and wins for humanity, or your gladiator glass shatters from an enemy's sword and your shards are left in a coliseum somewhere unknown.

It's not easy to be a glass gladiator hero with a pure heart who prays that G-D hears their voice in the arena and protects them as they engage in battle. Your hope is that He will give you the strength to fight on through your final moments.

Of note, it is Leonard (Cohen) who told Al that prior to his death to write something meaningful and heartfelt that will speak to generations.

Glass Gladiator is Al's *"Final Press Release"* and worthy to be set to a musical score and celebrated. Glass Gladiator will write its own media story for Motown's Glass Gladiator Press Officer.

May every Glass Gladiator's Shield and Sword protect and defend Humanity.)

Glass Gladiator
Lyrics by Al Abrams (September/October 2015)

The night is cold; the air is still. The earth lies frozen in the war chill.

My fingers, idly, trace your name across the snowy crumbling coliseum.

The stars look down so gray and dim; I close my eyes to see you in my dreams again. My glass armor is heavy; my sword stained with blood. I am G-D's Glass Gladiator fighting for freedom under His Flag.

Repairing the World is no simple task. I am not a caped hero with a supersonic past. I'm a simple Glass Gladiator who left my home to protect freedom for a world unknown.

The anthem of a Gladiator who is pure of heart is to do good in a world that is falling apart. Dust in a foreign land will be my fate my armor will shatter; my heart will not break.

*The World will listen to the shattering of glass and sing Hallelujah praise to a Gladiator's broken Glass.

Sword in hand, I took a stand for a noble quest called Freedom-Land.

Black and White lights flicker across the night sky. The concert of war raps in raging musical score.

A chord from the Gospel sings to my soul to keep fighting for freedom to bring every child home.
A darkened global coliseum is a Gladiator's fate. Palms or a Fall, it will resonate.

Not a noble hero; nor a shadow on a wall, only one of G-D's chosen band following His lead to the Promised Land.

*The World will listen to the shattering of glass and sing Hallelujah praise to a Gladiator's broken Glass.

All at once winter is gone; the mirage of a summer sun rises. I lay here dying without you lying beside me. Remembering when I walked with you across the field where flowers grew; and life renews.

I leave this weary world behind with you embedded in my summer mind. I feel you locked in my embrace as I softly touch your beautiful fading face.

I lay here lonely; Tears falling slowly. I recall what might have been if I didn't answer God's Gladiator's Song.

My armor is shattered; shards of glass on the ground. I am dying alone in a country coliseum unknown.

I recall how you loved me before you let me go – but know, that shards of my glass will always glow.
A Warrior's Blood runs Red; a Body turns to Dust. The Valor of a Gladiator is never lost, but victorious.

Celebrate my sword; it has fallen to my side. My glass armor is gone scattered on G-D's hallowed ground.

Love never dies; it always survives. It surrounds the clearing of global skies and humanity's eyes.

Celebrate me home as one of G-D's heroes … unknown.

*The World will listen to the shattering of glass and sing Hallelujah praise to a Gladiator's broken Glass

THE GLASS GLADIATOR
AL ABRAMS

The night is cold,
the air is still.
The frozen earth;
the warfare's chill.

Heavy armor, sword and blood
Freedom flag in foreign dust

My fingers, idly, trace your name
across the broken coliseum

The stars look down,
so gray and dim
I see you in my dreams again

Made of glass;
Left my home
To try to save a
world unknown.

To mend a world's
no simple task.
I'm no hero, no cape or mask

The anthem of the pure of heart
do good in a world that's come apart.

Foreign dust will be my fate
Glass may crack
but my heart won't break.

Black and White,
the concert of war.
Flashing lights in musical score.

A chord of Gospel sings to my soul
fighting to bring every child home.

A dark arena is a fighter's fate.
Palms or Fall, will resonate

No hero, no shadow,
G-D's chosen hand
follow His lead to the
Promised Land.

The WORLD will listen
to the SHATTERING GLASS
singing *Hallelujah* praise
To GLADIATORS past.

My armor shattered; dying alone
shards of glass, an arena unknown.
I recall you loved me then let me go
but, these shards of glass will always glow

Warrior Blood Running Red;
a body turns to Ash and Dust.
Gladiator's valor never lost,
The glass can glow victorious.

my sword has fallen to my side.
The shattered glass is hard to find.
But Love won't die; always survives
surrounds the clearing of global skies
A sight to see for humanity's eyes.
Celebrate me home as the ashes fly
one of G-D's heroes...unknown.

All at once winter's gone
Illusion of a summer sun
Shining as I lay here dying
without you by my side.

Thinking of a time I knew
Recalling when I walked with you
across the field where flowers grew
and once again will rise.

I leave this weary world behind
with you inside my summer mind
I feel you locked in my embrace
I softly touch your fading face

I lay here lonely, tears fall slowly
wonder what could be if only
I didn't answer G-D's Gladiator call.

(Graphic by Brandon Fields)

GLASS GLADIATOR

**Revision for Music Scoring March 11,2025
by Drew Schultz & Paul Riser Sr. – Motown)**

The night is cold; the air is still.
The frozen earth; the warfare's chill.

Heavy armor, sword and blood
Freedom flag in Foreign dust

My fingers, idly, trace your name
across the broken coliseum.

The stars look down so gray and dim
I see you in my dreams again.

*The World will listen to the shattering glass
singing Hallelujah praise to Gladiators past.

Made of glass; left my home
To try to save a world unknown.

To mend a world's no simple task.
I'm no hero, no cape or mask.

The anthem of the pure of heart
do good in a world that's come apart.

Foreign dust will be my fate
Glass may crack, but my heart won't break

*The World will listen to the shattering glass
singing Hallelujah praise to Gladiators past.

Black and White, the concert of war.
Flashing lights in musical score.

A chord of Gospel sings to my soul

fighting to bring every child home.

A dark arena is a fighter's fate.
Palms or Fall, will resonate.

No hero; no shadow, G-D's chosen band
follow His lead to the Promised Land.

*The World will listen to the shattering glass
singing Hallelujah praise to Gladiators past.

All at once winter's gone
Illusion of a summer sun
Shining as I lay here dying
without you by my side.

Thinking of a time I knew
Recalling when I walked with you
across the field where flowers grew
and once again will rise.

I leave this weary world behind
with you inside in my summer mind.
I feel you locked in my embrace
I softly touch your fading face.

I lay here lonely; Tears fall slowly.
wonder what could be if only
I didn't answer God's Gladiator call.

*The World will listen to the shattering glass
singing Hallelujah praise to Gladiators past.

My armor shattered; dying alone
shards of glass, an arena unknown.
I recall you loved me then let me go
but, these shards of glass will always glow.

Warrior Blood Running Red;

a Body turns to Ash and Dust.
Gladiator's valor never lost,
The glass can glow victorious.

My sword has fallen to my side.
The shattered glass is hard to find.
But Love won't die; always survives.
surrounds the clearing of global skies
A sight to see for humanity's eyes.
Celebrate me home as the ashes fly
one of G-D's heroes ... unknown.

*The World will listen to the shattering glass
singing Hallelujah praise to Gladiators past.

I Love the Way You Love
Lyrics written by Berry Gordy, Mike Ossman, **Al Abrams**, John O'Den

United Artist Record Star — MARV JOHNSON — Personal Management Berry Gordy, Jr.

It's what's in the grooves that count

Berry Gordy Jr 1962

It's what's in the words that count

Al Abrams 2011

1960's Motown Press Releases

from the Al Abrams Collection

ORIGINAL REMINGTON TYPEWRITER
AL ABRAMS - MOTOWN PRESS OFFICER
PRESS RELEASES-DOCUMENTS
1959 - 1967

Signature: *Al Abrams*

Date: 3 September 2013

March 18, 1965

FROM: Motown Record Corporation
       2648 West Grand Boulevard
       Detroit, Michigan 48208

For additional information
contact Al Abrams (TR 1-3340)

FOR IMMEDIATE RELEASE

SUPREMES BREAK THE RECORD

Detroit's Supremes, the nation's hottest new singing sensations, have shattered a long standing record by becoming both the first American vocal group, and the first female recording artists ever to have four consecutive number one recordings.

The record that did the trick for the Supremes, "STOP IN THE NAME OF LOVE" goes to number one in the nation as of Monday, March 22nd according to Billboard Magazine.

The only other recording artists to achieve this distinction have been England's Beatles. Even in their heyday, Elvis Presley and Fats Domino never quite made it four straight.

The Supremes; Diana Ross, Mary Wilson, and Florence Ballard, will celebrate their unprecedented honor while in London, England, where they are currently appearing with other top Detroit recording artists as part of THE TAMLA-MOTOWN REVUE package.

--30--

March 29, 1965

FROM: Motown Record Corporation
2648 West Grand Boulevard
Detroit, Michigan 48208

For additional information
contact Al Abrams (TR 1-3340)

<u>FOR IMMEDIATE RELEASE</u>

Marvin Gaye, popular Detroit singer, who was recently hospitalized suffering from pulminary congestion and nervous exhaustion, will make his first appearance since his illness over ABC-TV's "Shindig" on Wednesday April 7th. (The program is televised locally over WXYZ-TV, channel seven, at 8:30 P.M. E.S.T.)

Also appearing on the same show will be Martha and the Vandellas, the popular "Detroit Sound" group, who are riding high with their recording of "NOWHERE TO RUN", which is the nation's Number Nine best-selling record.

Gaye, who had been recuperating in Bermuda, will now begin to fulfill his schedule of personal appearance engagements for the month of April. Among those cancelled by his illness, was a night club engagement where he was booked as a replacement for the late Sam Cooke. Gaye's current recording "I'LL BE DOGGONE", is listed among the top 50 records in this week's Billboard. The same magazine last week announced that a poll of the nations disc jockeys had chosen Gaye as their favorite Rhythm and Blues male vocalist.

The contracts have now been signed for Detroit's Supremes to open a two week engagement at the world famous Copa nightclub in New York, beginning July 15th.

--30--

March 18, 1965

FROM: Motown Record Corporation
2648 West Grand Boulevard
Detroit, Michigan 48208

For additional information
contact Al Abrams (TR 1-3340)

FOR IMMEDIATE RELEASE

MARTHA AND THE VANDELLAS
TO MAKE NATIONAL TELEVISION DEBUT

Martha and The Vandellas, Gordy recording artists, whose record of "NOWHERE TO RUN" becomes the nation's number 12 best selling record according to Billboard Magazine, (as of Monday March 22nd) will make their national television debut on ABC-TV's "Shindig" on Wednesday, April 7th at 8:30 P.M. E.S.T.

"Shindig" is televised locally over WXYZ-TV (channel seven) in Detroit.

Martha (Reeves) and The Vandellas; Betty Kelly and Rosiland Ashford are currently touring England as part of the Tamla-Motown Revue. Last year the trio received a "GRAMMY" award, the recording industry's highest tribute, in recognition of the nomination of their recording of "HEAT WAVE" as one of 1963's best recordings.

Originally the background group on recordings by vocalist Marvin Gaye, the girls began recording on their own while Martha was employed as a secretary in the Detroit offices of Motown Recording Corporation. All three of the girls are native Detroiters.

---30---

FROM: Hitsville, U.S.A.
2648 West Grand Blvd.
Detroit, Michigan 48208
871-3340 (Al Abrams)

May 4, 1966

FOR IMMEDIATE RELEASE

U.S.O. HONORS SUPREMES
AS SERVICEMEN'S FAVORITE

Variety's statement that The Supremes are the Andrews Sisters of the Sixties never rang truer than last week, when the Detroit vocal trio received word that they had been voted the favorite vocal group of the U.S. Forces in Vietnam.

The Supremes, Diana Ross, Mary Wilson, and Florence Ballard received a plaque from the Saigon branch of the U.S.O. informing them of their latest - and perhaps greatest - tribute.

The plaque was the first presented by the U.S.O. to a female vocal group since the serviceman's organization honored the Andrews Sisters for four consecutive years during World War Two.

##############

November 23, 1964

FROM: Motown Record Corporation
        2648 West Grand Blvd.
        Detroit, Michigan 48208

For additional information contact:
        Al Abrams (TR. 1-3340)

FOR IMMEDIATE RELEASE

Lightning Strikes Thrice

Three young Detroit girls, the Supremes, have accomplished the remarkable feat of hitting the Number One spot on the national record charts twice within a few weeks. Their recording of "Baby Love", places them in line to receive their second Billboard magazine award, the first being for their recording of "Where Did Our Love Go", for which they received a gold record denoting sales of over a million records. In addition a third recording, "Come See About Me" is rapidly climbing the charts, and is listed as Number 13 in the current Billboard magazine.

The Supremes record of "Baby Love" is simultaneously Number One in both the United States and England. They are also the first American group to have two tunes in the British top twenty at one time, and they have made British disc history by becoming the first female vocal group ever to reach the Number One position in the New Musical Express charts, since it's inception in 1952.

The Supremes, Diana Ross, Mary Wilson and Florence Ballard, recently returned from a three week tour of England and Europe where their appearances on British television shows caused crowd scenes reminiscent of the Beatles reception in America.

-30-

February 15, 1965

FROM: Motown Record Corporation
        2648 West Grand Boulevard
        Detroit, Michigan, 48208

For additional information
contact: Al Abrams (TR 1-3340)

MARVIN GAYE REVUE
RETURNS TO 20 GRAND

Marvin Gaye, popular Detroit recording artist, opens a ten day engagement at Detroit's Club 20 Grand on Friday, February 19th. Featured on the bill with Marvin are: songstress Kim Weston, The Spinners, and the Earl Van Dyke Band. Last year a similiar show broke all existing house records for the 20 Grand according to owner, Bill Kabbush.

Negotiations are currently underway for Marvin Gaye to fulfill many of the nightclub engagements left open by the death of Sam Cooke. These include New York's Copacabana, and major Las Vegas and Miami Beach clubs. Tentative plans are also being made for Marvin to sing the Academy Award best song nominee "My Kind Of Town" on the national telecast of the Oscar presentations in April. "My Kind Of Town" is from the musical film "Robin And The Seven Hoods" which starred Frank Sinatra. The tune was recorded by Marvin in his best selling Tamla album "Hello Broadway".

-- 30 --

February 22, 1965

FROM: Motown Record Corporation
        2648 West Grand Boulevard
        Detroit, Michigan 48208

For additional information contact
Al Abrams (TR 1-3340)

FOR IMMEDIATE RELEASE

HARVARD-TYPE FOLK SINGER

OPENS AT DETROIT'S CHESSMATE

Booker Bradshaw, probably the only major folk singer to hold a Harvard Degree opens a 13 day engagement at Detroit's Chessmate Club beginning Tuesday, March 2nd. In addition to his Harvard education, Bradshaw studied at London's Royal Academy of Dramatic Art.

The young folk-singer and actor recently cut his first album for Detroit's Motown Records. Label president, Berry Gordy, Jr. is greatly enthused over the range of Bradshaw's ethnic folk material. Bradshaw's album marks Motown's entry into the area of folk music.

The Chessmate is located at McNichols and Livernois.

Show times at the unique folk club are: 9:30 PM, 11:00 PM; and midnight.

--30--

April 21, 1965

FROM: Motown Record Corporation
      2648 West Grand Boulevard
      Detroit, Michigan   48208

For additional information
contact Al Abrams (TR 1-3340)

FOR IMMEDIATE RELEASE

"DETROIT SOUND" ARTIST
ON NATIONAL TELEVISION

   The 4 Tops, popular Detroit vocal group, will appear on ABC-TV's "Shindig" on Wednesday, April 28. The show is televised locally over WXYZ-TV, channel seven, at 8:30 P.M. E.S.T.

--30--

March 29, 1965

FROM: Motown Record Corporation
      2648 West Grand Boulevard
      Detroit, Michigan   48208

For additional information
contact Al Abrams (TR 1-3340)

FOR IMMEDIATE RELEASE

SUPREMES WENT TO YALE: SO HARVARD WANTS MIRACLES

   Smokey Robinson and the Miracles, popular Detroit recording artists, are following in the footsteps of the Supremes, by entering the new frontier of personal appearances at the nations leading college campuses.

   The Miracles will perform at Harvard University in Cambridge, Massachusetts on May 14th. The Supremes recently appeared at Yale University and at Colby College in Waterville, Maine.

   The Miracles are currently touring England as part of the TAMLA-MOTOWN REVUE. Their new Tamla single "OOO BABY BABY" is quickly moving up the nation's best selling record lists.

   Bill "Smokey" Robinson, lead singer of the Miracles is also a well known songwriter; having written the recent Number One record "MY GIRL" for the Temptations. In addition, he is a Vice President of Motown Record Corporation.

--30--

September 29, 1965

FROM: Motown Record Corporation
2648 West Grand Boulevard
Detroit, Michigan 48208
For additional information contact
Al Abrams (TR 1-3340)

FOR IMMEDIATE RELEASE

Detroit's Supremes and Four Tops have been requested to headline the first show of "Pop" recording artists to entertain American soldiers in Vietnam. The Pentagon announced plans today for the 16 day tour which will run from January 6th through 22th, 1966.

The reason for the tour, according to a spokesman is that "Most of the troops over in Vietnam are about 19 or 20 years old. They would prefer to be entertained by their favorite popular recording artists such as the Supremes, and the Four Tops, rather than by performers with whom they do not identify".

The first "Pop" music show to entertain our troops will make a number of appearances in the Dominican Republic on October 8th, 9th, and 10th. The tour spokesman was quoted as saying "There are 13,000 Marines over in Santo Domingo who haven't had entertainment and they're getting mighty lonely. Detroit's Martha and The Vandellas have been requested to entertain on this tour.

Bob Parkinson (originally from Toledo, Ohio) the top-rated Washington D.C. disc jockey and Program Director of radio station W.E.A.M. will act as Master of Ceremonies for both tours.

Motown Recording Artist Brenda Holloway will make her nightclub debut at "It's Boss" (the former Ciro's) on Hollywood's famed "Sunset Strip" October 19th through 25th. Another Motown Artist, Billy Eckstine, will be appearing at the Elmwood Casino in Windsor, Ontario, Canada from October 29th through November 18th.

- 30 -

March 23, 1965

FROM: Motown Record Corporation
2648 West Grand Boulevard
Detroit, Michigan 48208

For additional information
contact Al Abrams (TR 1-3340)

FOR IMMEDIATE RELEASE

DETROIT RECORDING ARTISTS "TOPS" IN DISC JOCKEY POLL

Billboard Magazine's 1965 Disc Jockey Poll results show that the nation's record spinners like the "DETROIT SOUND" as much as the nation's record buyers.

In the overall pop category, Detroit's Supremes were chosen as the second favorite vocal group, behind the first place Beatles. Marvin Gaye was named the DJ's favorite rhythm and blues male singer, while the Temptations and the Supremes finished in first and second place respectively, in the favorite rhythm and blues group category.

In addition, a number of recordings by the Supremes, the Temptations, and other Detroit artists were chosen as 1965's best to date--in both the popular and rhythm and blues classifications. The "DETROIT SOUND" dominated the latter field with four out of the six winners.

The Supremes will make their New York night club debut at the world famous Copacabana in July.

The Temptations will headline a 10 day revue at Detroit's Club 20 Grand beginning April 30th.

--30--

FROM: Hitsville, U.S.A.
2648 West Grand Blvd.
Detroit, Michigan 48208
871-3340 (Al Abrams)

January 3, 1966

FOR IMMEDIATE RELEASE

MOTOWN NOW NUMBER ONE
IN U.S. SINGLE RECORD SALES

Detroit's Motown Record Corporation is now Number One in total single record sales for the year of 1965. (According to Billboard Magazine tabulations).

Motown came up from Fourth place in 1963 to Second in 1964 to the then leader in single sales, Capitol Records, which holds U.S. rights to all recordings by the Beatles.

Founded in 1958 by former auto assembly worker, Berry Gordy Jr., Motown has grown to become the largest independent record manufacturer in the United States. Motown has given Detroit a new worldwide fame as the home of "The Detroit Sound" group of top record artists, THE SUPREMES, MARVIN GAYE, THE FOUR TOPS, STEVIE WONDER, THE TEMPTATIONS and others.

The charts which showed the Top Ten Records of 1965 did not contain any Beatles recordings, as compared to 1964 when the Beatles dominated the charts.

The chart of 1965's Top Ten Records, show three Motown recordings among the Top Ten.

No. 1 - "Back In My Arms Again" - The Supremes (MOTOWN)
No. 2 - "Wooly Bully" - Sam The Sham and The Pharos
No. 3 - "Mr. Lonely" - Bobby Vinton
No. 4 - "I Can't Help Myself" - The Four Tops (MOTOWN)
No. 5 - "Satisfaction" - The Rolling Stones
No. 6 - "Downtown" - Petula Clark
No. 7 - "You've Lost That Lovin' Feeling" - Righteous Brothers
No. 8 - "Come See About Me" - The Supremes (MOTOWN)
No. 9 - "The In Crowd" - Ramsey Lewis
No. 10 "You Were On My Mind" - The We Five

1965 was a bad year for the Beatles.

A closer relationship between the Beatles and Motown is in the works. The Beatles have already requested that the team of Holland-Dozier-Holland, who have written and produced all of THE SUPREMES and FOUR TOPS' Number One Records, to write two songs especially for the Beatles.

The Beatles special 1965 Christmas and New Years record, which is sent only to their fans and is not available for airplay or for sale, features the Beatles singing Holland-Dozier-Holland's "It's The Same Old Song" popularized by Motown's FOUR TOPS.

THE SUPREMES' upcoming album "I Hear A Symphony features a song entitled "Yesterday", as written by the Beatles' Lennon and McCartney. THE SUPREMES' new single, "My World is Empty Without You" (by Holland-Dozier-Holland) is also featured in the album.

2

Motown Man of Valor - Your Brother in Arms

Bernie Yeszin came into my life at a time when I needed a friend. He was more than a friend; he was a mentor, a guide, and a beacon of light. Bernie helped save me from myself in countless ways and set me on a path that enabled me to become my very best self.

As an artist, Bernie was unmatched. His creativity and vision positively impacted and improved everyone and everything he encountered. Whether interacting with humans, dogs, or any other beings, his influence was profound and transformative. Despite his many awards and accolades, Bernie was never truly fully appreciated or understood by the rest of the world because he was so far ahead of his time. His masterful communication and artistic prowess set him apart, making him a true visionary.

As a person, Bernie was kind, caring, generous, and considerate. He enjoyed sharing his knowledge not just about animals, but about art and the finer things in life. He taught me about KINSHIP WITH ALL LIFE, the very notion of which has changed me as a person forever. He also taught me to keep my circle small and to have pride in myself and my work to a degree beyond what I already knew. He helped me harness all of my focus and abilities to execute a singular vision.

One of the greatest joys of my life was forming Dog Stars Inc. with Bernie and collaborating with him on "Bernie and Daisy's 3D Circus." This project pushed the limits of stereoscopic 3D filmmaking combined with delightful performances. He believed in me, inspired me, and changed me in ways that impact me daily. Not a day goes by that I don't recall a lesson or utilize something he instilled in me, and that is the true definition of friendship. That is the telltale sign of a friend.

James Markham Hall, Jr.
Co-Founder, CEO - Gold Creek VR
http://www.GoldCreekVR.com

NOWHERE TO RUN - MOTOWN, HOLLYWOOD & 'NAM

Al & NC Abrams
Bernie Yeszin Graphic by Brandon Daniels

My attic mate, Bernie Yeszin, Motown Art Director, has always been excluded from Motown History.

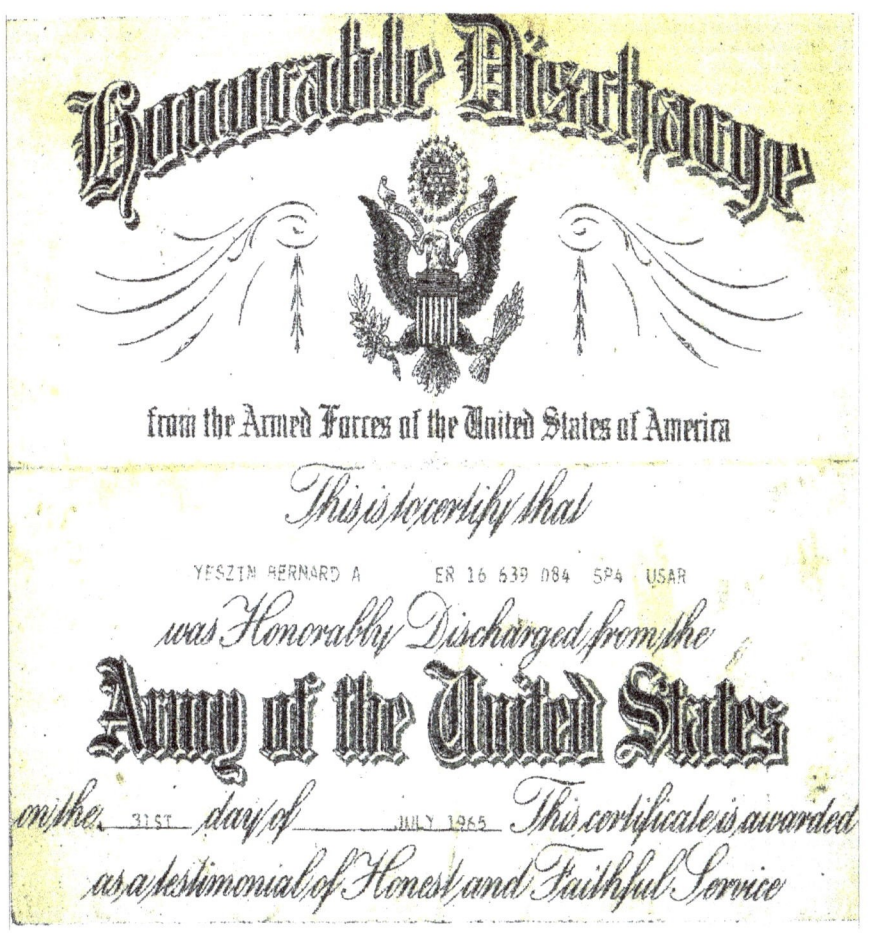

"Nowhere to run to baby, Nowhere to hide" blared over loudspeakers in every Vietnam jungle encampment where U.S. soldiers checked their weapons for another round in casino combat hell. Rolling the reality dice to survive became a 24/7 war game.

A five-pointed terrazzo and brass Star embedded in Hollywood's Walk of Fame sidewalks at Hollywood & Vine features the names of Motown artists and many stars that have only played onscreen movie soldiers.

Inscribed on a slab of solid black granite, "The Waif', on the National Mall, Washington DC is where the names of real Stars are honored for their commitment to country through their courage and sacrifice in America's divisive politicized foreign war.

The three worlds of Motown, Hollywood and 'Nam collided in a unique way when two young Jewish guys, far from Hollywood & Vine, first met in a Black-owned Detroit record label's 3rd floor attic located in a house on West Grand Boulevard in Detroit. It became their "Hitsville" office, affectionately known as ABA - Al & Bernie - The Attic.

Both grew up in a Jewish enclave in America's heartland. They attended different Detroit public high schools. Bernie attended Mackenzie High School (Demolished, 2012). Al attended Central High School.

Bernie Yeszin became Motown's talented Art Director. He created more than 200 mesmerizing Motown album covers. His first album cover was for Martha & The Vandellas, Come and Get These Memories. He is also responsible for designing the distinctive and iconic Motown "M" logo as is seen by millions. It graces album covers, film credits, TV specials, t-shirts and was even projected on Berry Gordy's Motown: The Musical Broadway New York curtains.

Al Abrams became Motown's incredible Press Officer. He put the Motown hype into press releases, liner notes, ghosted stories in teen magazines and created the aura of excitement surrounding Berry Gordy and Motown artists. He even enticed TV guide to place the Supremes on their cover. It was a breakthrough for African Americans. Al gave Motown its famous crossover slogan, Motown: the Sound of Young America and The Detroit Sound. Later, Al gave Stax-Volt, The Memphis Sound slogan.

Together, this team became known as Motown's crazy creative duo. Bernie even created a sign for their attic space informing visitors they had to sing to enter.

Their poignant and powerful story centers on a lifetime friendship melded through their love of music, respect for each other and a very personal and private secret that Bernie kept when he was a Motowner.

Bernie's Secret: He became an American Teen GI and served in a war sometimes referred to as "The American War". He was not alone. Other post high school graduates followed the same U.S.-Vietnamese military footprint to Indochina. Hell awaited their boots on the ground.

Bernie conscripted and, honorably, served in the U.S. Army as one of the first soldiers sent to Vietnam. His honorable discharge papers reflect his character.

A naive teenage boy sent into a grown up war never returns emotionally or physically without deep scarring. Oftentimes, if they make it home alive, repressed memories of war, even years later, can eventually become a soldier's death knell.

Vietnam became the unscripted decades old movie playing as a rerun inside Bernie's head. Al became his trusted war correspondent.

Bernie would recall the U.S. military dropping Agent Orange, a herbicide and defoliant chemical for its tactical purposes. The military goal was to defoliate the rural and forested lands used to feed and give cover to guerrillas. Soldiers were never informed of its deadly human and environmental effects.

And then there were the phosphorus grenades that were used to destroy Viet Cong tunnels. The grenades would burn up the oxygen in the tunnel and suffocate the enemy combatants hiding inside. The tunnel escape hatch would be blocked to prevent escape. The sound of human cries, coughing and knowing that human flesh was piling up inside had to be accepted as a consequence of war.

While Bernie had put his teenage combat boots on the ground in 'Nam, Al was working to get White Deejays to spin some Black Motown on their turntables.

The turbulent and fiery 1960s played under a play list of Motown music that saw teenage sock hop dance floors become integrated.

DJ's streamed the crossover music over radio airwaves all over the world, including Vietnam. Songs: My Girl; Please Mr. Postman; Reach Out I'll Be There; Jimmy Mack; Stop in the Name of Love; My Guy; Heat Wave; The Tracks of My Tears; Don't Mess With Bill ... Motown's Sixties record hits were part of the music that allowed a Movement to happen without ever having, initially, joined any Movement.

Bernie and Al were both advocates for civil rights and justice. Working for Motown allowed them entrance into a rather elite clubhouse where the color of skin did not exclude you from becoming part of a family where music always started and ended the conversation.

Al explained to Bernie that Vietnam was extremely political and polarizing. Motown did not want to take a stance. Discussing Vietnam was considered off-limits.

In fact, Motown would spin itself away from anything that might cause record sales to plummet and cut into its profit margins. Thus, it disconnected itself from every possible distraction that labeled itself as a "Movement". (Later Motown changed its tune thanks to Marvin Gaye who wanted the country to know, What's Going On.)

There is a caveat to Gordy's real vs. toy soldier view. Al, privately, informed Gordy that one of his employees, Michael Roshkind, was masquerading as a military hero and "Stealing Valor". Gordy, didn't fire Roshkind. Instead, Gordy moved his fake toy soldier with him to LA and promoted him to President of Motown.

REAL VETERAN - NO! TOY SOLDIER- YES!

The Boys, finally, grew up and moved out of the Motown family house and left behind their Attic office and the music memories made there. However, their friendship was never left on West Grand Boulevard. It was etched in their hearts.

Neither of their names will be found on a star studded Hollywood street. They were the behind-the-scene unknown guys linked to Motown's history, its success and mystique. Their names and contributions to Motown history made in the Hitsville Family attic is yet to be recognized.

Bernie slathered on suntan lotion donned a pair of Aviator sunglasses and went Hollywood. He found work as an Art Director for movie and television sets. He went on to win an Emmy for his Art Direction for the Tracy Ullman Show.

However, when art direction jobs became scarce he traded in his eye for design to train dogs. Bernie with his dog, Daisy, won Animal Planet's "Who Let The Dogs Out" TV show. He even wrote a dog training book.

His best friend became his beautiful Golden Retriever, Daisy. But, Bernie, also, had one underlying 'Nam mental condition (PTSD) that plagued and infected his entire life. America was trying to forget Vietnam. The veterans who lived it were traumatized the minute they LZ'd (landing-zoned) onto Vietnam soil.

Al crossed the border into Canada and became a journalist for the Windsor Star Newspaper where he went on to win a Western Ontario Newspaper Award for Investigative Reporting. (It is equivalent to a Pulitzer Prize without the public adulation and dollars.) Al's best friend was a cat named Ketz.

Miles separated these two friends for decades, but their friendship and that secret shared in their Motown attic hideaway brought their 1960s friendship and the 'Nam war games replaying inside Bernie's head to an internalized secret called "Soldier Shame".

Bernie was embarrassed, humiliated and homeless. He and his loyal Daisy were surviving in a broken down 1990 GMC Suburban overlooking Hollywood for a couple of years. His possessions, minus one pawned, then gone Emmy, filled the interior of his vehicle.

During the day, the intense LA sun bore down on the Suburban; at night, it became a cramped bed. The nearby LA River allowed Bernie and Daisy a chance to bathe. Oftentimes, as night fell, Bernie was harassed and threatened by roving violent gangs out for some high-kicks.

Cheap alcohol, drugs and his dedicated Daisy became Bernie's round the clock companions.

Who could a former soldier that stumbles and fall down reach out to that wouldn't judge them for losing out to the warriors playing X-Box war games inside their head?

He desperately needed to send an SOS to his Motown Family Attic mate. Bernie found a local Hollywood copy shop with computer access. He sent an incoherent email to Al with a cell phone number.
Al responded without hesitation. Bernie and Al spoke for a few hours reminiscing about Motown and their buried history.
What Al didn't tell Bernie is that he was scheduled to leave for New York City that evening for a "Special Pre-Opening Night" invitation for Motown Family to attend Gordy's self-influenced, Motown: The Musical. Bernie's Invite: MIA
Ironic, Bernie's beautifully designed "M' logo would be gracing the curtains on a Broadway stage; yet, Motown's unrecognized artistic soldier boy who designed it was still in LA reliving the visuals of a forgotten war without a curtain call or applause.

The conversation eased into Bernie's SOS to Al.

Bernie skidded from remembering playing ice hockey on the Detroit River; deployment to Vietnam; becoming part of the "Motown Family"; winning a coveted TV Emmy; and playing with dogs.

He always returned to the stench, visuals, and sounds relevant to 'Nam that he experienced as a young man. War always leaves the battlefield within a soldier's head.

Bernie needed immediate help. The Suburban needed to be repaired and new plates purchased. He wanted to find a safe place for himself, Daisy and another dog. He needed professional help to, finally, cope with his Vietnam movie. Bernie made it clear that the LA VA Hospital was not an option. It was the kiss of death for any veteran walking through its doors.

True friendship is non-judgmental. War is judgmental, controversial and, always, political. Motown, sidestepped, Vietnam to sell records. Gordy promoted a guy who "Stole Valor" yet, would rebuff a "Motown Family" member who served their country.

No. Al didn't go to NYC to attend Motown: The Musical. Instead, he got Bernie the help he needed to try to resuscitate the life that had been drained from him as a naive nineteen-year-old trying to cope with life after high school graduation.

There is so much more to the Attic Mates of Motown story.

In July, 2014 Bernie succumbed to the physical and emotional battles raging inside him. He died in a public hospital in Culver City, CA. Al made his final arrangements. (Daisy also passed.)

Unfortunately, in October 2015, Al, followed his friend to a Cloud Nine Attic Office.

Bernie used to sign off in his emails to Al with: "Luv, Your Brother-In-Arms"; Al would sign off with a simple, "Cheers".

The non-Motown song, "Impossible Dream" is an appropriate ending to the music played in an attic bunker on West Grand Blvd and a lifetime friendship where the music played in the background.

"This is my quest, to follow that STAR No matter how hopeless, No matter how far ... To fight for the right Without question or pause To be willing to march into hell for a heavenly cause".

*"lmpossible Dream" song composer, Mitch Leigh; lyrics written, Joe Darion.

NOTE: Hitsville (Motown Museum) and its Multi-Million Dollar Renovations ... Where is the ABA - The Al-Bernie, 3rd Floor Attic Boys Space where the Motown historical PRESS and ART for a Black owned record company was created?

Al did reach out to the Gordy Foundation to help Bernie. He had hoped that the Motown Family would help one of the Family. REPLY ... Nothing.

Al, then, reached out to MusiCares. MusiCares stepped in without hesitation and helped where the Motown Family failed him. Al, also, used his own resources to insure that Bernie got help in the final days of his life and a proper sendoff.

Thank you MusiCares.

EMAIL EXCHANGES BETWEEN BERNIE & AL
(Decades After Leaving Motown)

Bernard Yeszin
      i am your ol' mt mate @ 70 yrs ol' would you believe

Bernard Yeszin
      Al baby   Please call me very very important -------love call man call Your Brother in arms …

Bernard Yeszin yez

Al baby,

Wouldn't you know that when I left MT I, (wanting to do the right thing) compiled all the Art Depts. artwork, photos, layouts, drawing etc. into a neat
and accessible bundle (file) and left it for the next A.D. Even covers I designed that had not been put out yet and were later released with someone else's credit or none at all.

Your Brother in Arms, B

Bernard Yeszin
Re: Things that go round and round

I get asked all the time from all kinds of sources for my old record business stuff. Oh yea, Esther Edwards herself actually took credit for some subsequent covers of mine after I left. She up-surged Berry of seeing over the Art Dept., that and the fact she wouldn't give me the raise that I deserved.
I am miserable, broke and need a job. Can do commissioned paintings ...but I don't have a studio. Maybe you know someone who can provide me with space?

Thanks for hanging in with me. Need you.
Your Brother in Arms – B

Bernard Yeszin
Chrysler wears my LOGO

The article should have had the headline "The Man Behind the Motown Logo Steps Out in Front to Paint a Masterpiece"
Have you seen the new Chrysler 300 Motown Edition with my logo on the side?

Bernard Yeszin

Al
The early years, those halcyon years, are the years that define MT. Yet it was I who forced down the throats of the Gordys' the MT logo. Talk about "branding" 50 years later that logo is still in force today. fyi that design actually represented the 3 little houses of which was and will always be the iconic Motown. It was I who changed the image of those 3 young girls into the sophisticated lookin' ladies. It was I who for $5 a night and gas money, sometimes drove "the girls" as you did, to their record hops in the dead of winter of 62 63 64.
It was I who put the Temptations in white suits to create the Temptin' Temps. The Vandellas "HeatWave" album cover shall always be remembered as MT's finest album cover, ask anybody. Talk about image, how about the Miracles "Goin' to a-Go-Go", what a look.
I carry the letter with me all the time of a detailed letter from Martin Luther King thanking me for the covers I did for his March on Washington speech, as well as the Detroit speech.
Those Friday morning meetings in Mr Gordy's office were always opened with me presenting my work in progress that week, I set the tone for that meeting , as well as a

1/10 vote on every thing to be released. You were there pen in hand.

My close friendship with Marvin Gaye I shall cherish always, we remained friends throughout his life.

My contribution will never be recognized, say-la-vie.

I carry with me hundreds of interesting annotates, of which MT devoted fans would love to hear, but alas my dear friend Al, it shall never be. My role will never see the light of day

Hey it was Tommy Good and I who were foot-stomps, hand-claps, and finger -pops on "Where Did Our Love Go"

Warm regards – Bro in Arms, B

Bernard Yeszin

Lots of friends at MT Martha, Paul Riser, Lawrence, Billie Jean, Betty Edwards, Phil Jones, All the Spinners (when they all worked in the shipping dept)

A year ago I had stored for safekeeping 6 boxes of my personal belonging at a friends photo studio (I was in transit at the time). When I went to retrieve my stuff there was only 5 boxes remaining. I and my friend surmised one of clients probably stole it. The missing box contained all my music cds (about 200), all my art supplies (3 doz. or so new brushes, several hundred dollars of oil paint and a stack of art books.

I immediately made a police report and is on record. Much later, I discovered to my dismay the awful fact that my beloved Emmy was also in that box. I DID NOT GO BACK TO THE POLICE TO AMEND the error. as I felt all was lost and still is. This morning I went to the police dept to get a copy of the report, even though the Emmy was not included. The copy would take at least 6weeks to get. The report # is 11 06 18945.

      The Emmy has been a touchstone for me and miss it dearly. I get a lot of joy when folks can't
help themselves from picking it up and thanking the Academy and every one they know. I am about to maybe return to my home-town of Detroit, Michigan (I
am retired) and I would like very much like to have
that ol' touchstone with me to show with pride my greatest accomplishment.
All the best Your Brother in Arms,
Bernie

From: Bernard Yeszin

Update & Favor – Al – Thank you and your wife for saving me right now. You married a good woman who is compassionate to me a homeless and sick stranger.

What has Motown ever done for me? Gave me you my friend – We are the overlooked creative team that Motown deletes from its history as if we never existed. We were hid in an attic. I did the art and you did the press. We were damn good my attic mate.

Bernard Yeszin

I'm thinking this is not going well. I'm not looking forward to rejection from Mr Gordy, it would hurt dearly.

I appreciate your effort but ... Motown won't help me but you, my friend, are still trying.

it's breaking my heart i don't think I can stand it, the thought that people will actually read this story about me has sent me in a deep depression and now that the story is out I shall hide my head in despair and disappear. Why people get joy from reading of others downward spiral gives credence to my cynicism. The article should have been of hope. I hate myself for exposing my shame. Please do your best to nix the story or just let it die of its own accord. And please do your best NOT to have Mary Wilson see it as she has always been the hidden desire of my life. Al I love you but as this dirty homeless sickly looking failure you do your self no favor by your association. Your honest effort has not
gone unappreciated.

From: Al

Subject: Motown the Musical Alumni Invitation for April 5 NYC

Bernie:

How are things with you; all the dogs and Daisy? Hope things will improve for all of us old timers in 2013. Quick question for you.

Have you been tracked down and sent an invitation to *Motown the Musical* for a special Motown alumni performance to be held on April 5 in NYC. The invite provides the alumnus with two tickets to the

Broadway performance and includes a post cocktail reception after the show. Soulful Detroit - MOTOWN FORUM had something on it asking who made the list of invitees for the Friday, April 5 alumni event?

It was also in Brian McCullom's column in the *Detroit Free Press* as a blurb in his *Motown Notebook* column.

Hope all is better in LA. I'll keep you in my prayers and will continue to help where I can.

Let me know.

Also, maybe you and Daisy could attend in tux and a Supreme's - like ball gown. Still a PR guy here ... always thinking as to how to grab those headlines.

Cheers!

  Bernard Yeszin

I'm thinking this is not going well. I'm not looking forward to rejection from Mr Gordy, that would hurt dearly, as I have respect for the man. I appreciate your effort but -
From: Al
Subject: Options

Bernie:

I hope you and Daisy are okay.

Don't shoot the messenger, but here are a couple of options subsequent to our phone calls.

For some strange reason, Lamont simply doesn't remember you. Beats me as to why. But his wife did come up with some information on a shelter that would take in both you and Daisy. Do you want me to forward it?

Kerry Gordy claims Raynoma has never mentioned you so he is also useless.

BUT -- if all goes well, I will see Berry in New York at his play on Friday, April 5. Do you want me to slip him a note with your phone number?

Do you want me to reach out to Tommy Good? He is an absolutely great guy.

I know how you feel about reaching out to your family, but with your permission, I would be glad to make the call to your sister.

There are other options too, but nothing happens without your prior approval. I understand.

I like your idea about making money by doing signed art reproductions of your classic covers. If we can find you a studio in which to work, provide the materials required, we can and will help you sell them.

Just don't give up hope. We'll find something yet.

Please call in any emergency - day or night.

Stay safe,
Al

Bernard Yeszin

it's breaking my heart i don't think I can stand it, the thought that people will actually read this has sent me in a deep depression and now the story is out I shall hide my head in despair and disappear . Why people get joy from reading of others downward spiral gives credence to my cynicism. The article should have been of hope. I hate myself for exposing my shame. Please do your best to nix the story or just let it die of its own accord. And please do your best NOT to have Mary Wilson see it as she has always been the hidden desire of my life. Al I love you but as this dirty homeless sickly looking failure you do your self no favor by your association. Your honest effort has not gone unappreciated though, one day maybe I can show you . How about a portrait of a loved one

---

God -Damn-It, if I don't have a Red Wing shootin" pucks on a frozen over Detroit River.   just as I did back in the the early 50's.
Your brother in arms
LV bERNIE

Bernard Yeszin
The story is actually half true as I did lose a box of my valuables.

if I have to make a new police report I would have to what? I don't have the nerve. Forgot my Emmy was being held by a dentist until I could get it back. I just don't know how I could return to Detroit without it, as all would be anxious to see it.

Re: Fwd: Forgotten Motown Alumni

Bernard Yeszin

How in the frigging hell does one forget the mighty ....Motown of course

-----Original Message-----
From: Al
Sent: Tue, Apr 30, 2013
Subject: Forgotten Motown Alumni

There seems to be names missing from the comprehensive Motown alumni list that has been available for online viewing since November 2012.

Al Abrams
Michael McLean
Bernard Yeszin

alan abrams minynsta friend to z endz

Z future is bleak to say the least
I contacted at least 6 trademark attorneys as to the MT logo on 50,000 dollar cars, I am
enraged, deranged basically my life is in
its saddest state and this has capped the very end of a career based on giving my best
As an employee one would think in a just society that talent will out. this artist has been stripped of any joy that may come from doing a rightest (kosher) job. I'm sick and now totally disengaged in the pursuit. The deck is stacked against me (as one lawyer stated)

Bernard Yeszin

  Here it is: the MT logo is now eclipsing the Detroit Tigers logo as the unofficial symbol of the motor city. It stands as hope as to the future aspirations of America itself. The GE logo, Kellogg's, Coca Cola. Ford, Nike,CBS,Fox. you get the picture. The logo-graph itself, one day, will stand as a 30 story building. It has personal impact on every one worldwide , even Barack himself (I'm sure)is motivated by it. and ,god bless his little soul, engraved on Mr Gordy's tomb.
My uncle Harry worked at Plymouth. My uncle Shine (never knew his 1st name) worked at Dodge.

When I saw the commercial I was oh so touched that the Temptin'Temps were wearing their white suits. The white fucking suits I insisted they have made for the cover. My work at MT was visceral. The package … what

would a Cadillac be without a Body by Fisher,
or ketcup without Heinz 57…

Hopefully musicares comes up with the dough I need for the suv, fix her up and a beeline to San Clem.   Beach bum.
      B w/lv

Those swashbucklers at la week….eat it …
And here goes, do not forward a word of the
blog….promise me AL

Bernard Yeszin

Al Baby
…..........forwarded all my dog show material to you for all your very influential, intelligent, hip, slick and cool people or to anyone who you think ever knew me, liked me, despised me, or just plain loves the canine race.
do you ever make it to LA?
Your Brother in Arms

Bernie & Daisy

Bernie with Jaime Hall & Daisy

334 Auburn Ave., N.E.
Atlanta, Georgia 30303
Telephone 524-1378

Southern Christian Leadership Conference

Martin Luther King Jr., *President*   Ralph Abernathy, *Treasurer*   Wyatt Tee Walker, *Executive Assistant*

September 23, 1963

Mr. Bernard Yeszin
2648 West Grand Boulevard
Detroit 8, Michigan

Dear Mr. Yeszin:

    Your recent thoughtful letter of encouragement and support in our efforts to bring about racial justice to all Americans is very much appreciated. You may be confident that such reassurance provides us with an additional source of strength and for this reason, if there were no other, I am deeply grateful.

    The commitment of all Americans to justice and brotherhood takes on new and even more imperative significance in the wake of the tragic deaths of the children in a Birmingham Sunday School class last week.

    There are numerous reasons which prompt me to express my appreciation to you. The personal commitments of all of us associated with the Southern Christian Leadership Conference is to the philosophy of nonviolence and redemptive love. I personally am convinced that this philosophy will enable all Americans to realize more fully their real potential as human beings. We seek to develop a climate of understanding and love in this nation which will enable all of our citizens to practice in their daily lives the true brotherhood of man and the fatherhood of God.

    To implement this type of conviction, it is necessary to eliminate all vestiges of racial injustice and discrimination. We are convinced that the proper method to seek the attainment of these goals is by nonviolent action only after all other constructive efforts through dialogue and negotiation have failed. We believe that this new society which we seek so fervently is now on the way to coming into being.

    Meantime, I beseech you to continue to engage your energies, intelligence and personal physical being in behalf of this social revolution which will prove to be a cleansing process for the entire American community.

    May the richest of blessings descend upon you and your loved ones.

                                           Sincerely yours,

                                           Martin Luther King, Jr.

MLK:r

9125 Rehco Road, San Diego, California 92121
(858) 453-7845 FAX (858) 453-6585

Mr. Bernard Yetzin
c/o Henry Aguilar
437 W. 54th St.
Los Angeles, CA 90037

April 13, 2012

Dear Mr. Yetzin,

On behalf of the entire team at Natural Balance, congratulations to you and Daisy for capturing the hearts of America and winning first place in the *Who Let the Dogs Out* national search for the most talented dogs in America. Please find enclosed a $500 gift card for Petco as part of your prize package which includes a one-year supply of Dick Van Patten's Natural Balance pet food, four nights at the Petco Pooch Hotel in Hollywood, and a $500 Petco gift card.

We look forward to seeing you and Daisy at your local Petco and on the season finale of *Who Let the Dogs Out* airing on Animal Planet!

Best Wishes,

Kathy Hughes
Product Marketing Manager
Petco Animal Supplies

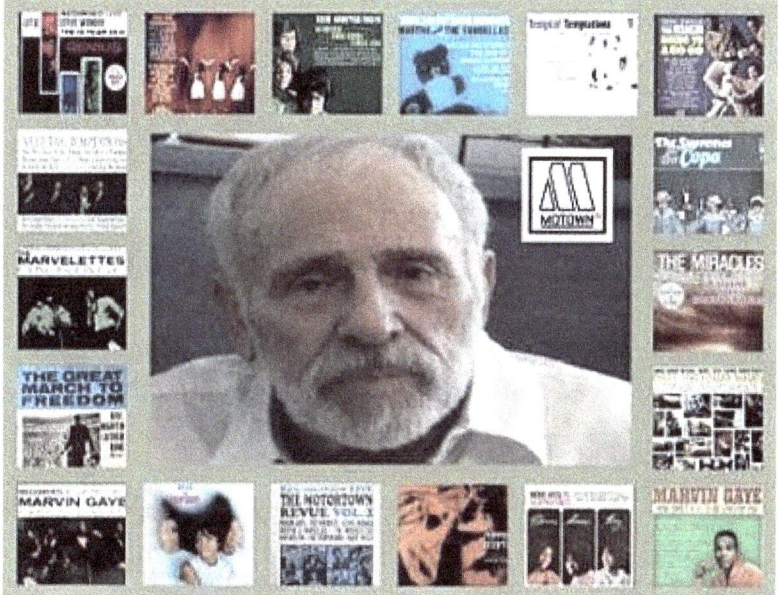

Bernie wins an OSCAR for Art Direction, Tracey Ullman Show

Iconic MOTOWN "M" Logo created by Motown Art Director Bernie Yeszin

3

Stolen Valor – D-Day Torpedo - Bury the Manuscript

Tik-Kum-Olah
Repair the World

Show me one-hundred gladiator heroes and heroines and I'll show you ninety-nine tragedies. Becoming a hero has consequence.

Ninety-nine tragedies left to die on any battlefield they did not choose will never tell their story. The only surviving hero or heroine becomes both the narrator and the story.

High School & College Graduation: 1968   The year of heroes by their 'Nam number. Male birthdates became America's political hope of winning a non-declared military war by the involuntary mass recruitment of young men into the armed services. The Vietnam War story has changed over time.

Inflate, deflate, deflect, create - history is, eventually, and always will be manipulated and revised.

Segregation, integration and Civil Rights flames were still smoldering in America's '68 urban and rural landscapes.

There is no simple solution to resolving global human rights issues, inequality and injustice wherever they are embedded. Landmines are buried in every country.

Music opens generational world conversations.

Activism is a desolate and uncertain pathway for every altruistic hero.

A hero is not destined to become a hero by birthright or education, nor defined by social class or wealth. And, clearly, donating to a charitable organization is not sacrificing and upending your life for a notable cause.

Most heroes are invisible and go unnoticed as they walk on any given street in the world. Activated by conscience, morality or circumstance is what determines their hero status.

Hundreds of heroes live in our world. They are the ordinary, non-caped crusaders that open a door; jumpstart a car; hand $ to a street beggar; give a ride to a stranded motorist; visit an elderly neighbor; teach a child to read; or donate to a charity.

However, there are those intuitive individuals in this global galaxy who are the caped crusaders that make us want to believe that good will ultimately win over evil as visualized in Hollywoodesque produced movies.

These individuals are willing to sacrifice their own livelihood, family and life for the greater good in our world and universe.

Soldiers and law enforcement officers defend us; whistleblowers challenge for us; "real" investigative journalists are jailed for us; spies infiltrate to protect us; social activists go under ground for us; and religious leaders place G-d first for us.

The menagerie of global heroes and their altruism for the greater good and truth is what ultimately and universally creates these super heroes into less fictional characters and movie mirages and more like the caped wonder men and women we applaud.

Every country has them. Every country needs them. Music connects heroes to us.

The YEAR: 1968 "Nowhere To Run ... Nowhere To Hide" ... blares on the radio. Motown: The Sound of Young America.

The song recorded by Martha Reeves & The Vandellas, an African-American female group, was adopted by a diverse group of young soldiers facing combat together.
The purity of the song's lyrics are as relevant today as they were in 1968.

It's about heroism and the music that defines it. Music is influential. Music is a universal language.Putting on a cape to Right a wrong is courageous. Humanity needs more heroes.

However, Berry Gordy would not listen to me as his confidant and media guy and hear what I discovered about his east coast cosmopolitan media hire – Michael Roshkind.

Gordy wanted the Detroit to Hollywood Halo and eventually awarded Roshkind a Motown "Presidential" Medal for not serving his country and lying about earning a military award for valor.

Michael Roshkind stated to media when confronted that he had awarded himself the Navy Cross to make himself a hero. He, also, stated that he was not proud of stealing real military valor. When asked whether he would contact Who's Who and revise his statement about his being awarded a Medal of Valor he basically replied that he had no interest in any change. So, the fabrication of being awarded the highest honor that can be bestowed upon military valor was for him to continue his lie and "Steal Valor".

The Navy Cross is the United States Naval Service's **second-highest military decoration.** It is awarded for sailors and marines who distinguish themselves for extraordinary heroism in combat with an armed enemy force.

Unfortunately, Motown never addressed this, truly, dishonorable "Stolen Valor" lie.

I was angered at Berry for not demanding a public retraction by Roshkind. Motown Family members served in our United States military, including Berry.

To me, disrespecting our military men and women by not confronting the Roshkind lie created an unfortunate music sin that has never been repaired by addressing it.

I know its decades later, but on behalf of my Motown Music Family, I want to publicly apologize to the United States Military men and women for this false claim of receiving a "Medal of Valor" by a Motown guy who, eventually, was promoted to President of Motown.

Motown has "Nowhere to Run; Nowhere to Hide from this Historical Fact.

From Stolen Valor to my personalized Motown D-Day Torpedo to wanting to bury my Motown Memoir manuscript did not prepare me for the ongoing Roshkind saga that imploded Motown's roots of being a "Motown Family" based music record label.

I was Motown's Press Officer during some of America's most perilous and dangerous history moments - Civil Rights Movement, Vietnam War, Kennedy Assassination and more.

I, as Motown's front media man, created the slogans that identified Motown: The Detroit Sound and Motown: The Sound of Young America. Also, after leaving Motown I had Stax labeled as The Memphis Sound when I was their media consultant. Almost all the Motown artists remained my friends after I left.

I discovered that the Motown website had a listing of Motown Family members. My name did not appear on that list. It, also, excluded other names. I contacted Hitsville with a list of Motown Family names MIA from their posted list.

How did I leave Motown … I got a call at my mother's home on December 7, 1966.

It was Berry's nouveau white executive, Michael Roshkind, who ingratiated himself to Berry. He told Berry that I was no longer needed at Motown as Motown needed more Hollywood Glitz and Glamour associated with it. And, that I was, basically, understand that Motown was now a success story that required a press guy with more polish, credentials and west coast connections.

I was hired by Gordy in 1959. Berry became like a big brother to me. He gave me clothing from his closet. He even learned some Yiddish to communicate with my mother. We had many fun and interesting escapades together. My commitment to Berry, Motown and all its artists helped Motown achieve its success. He even gave me his expensive Leica Camera so that I could back up photos. Yet, I was now expendable.

I had angered Berry by questioning Roshkind's credentials and resume and Berry's justifiable reasoning for hiring an enforcer-type individual.

I answered the Roshkind call. First words he said was for me to look out the front window. Roshkind had his car window rolled down. His hand was out and he had it pointed like a gun at me. He said, "You've been torpedoed". Your fired and don't call Berry. He rolled up his window and drove away.

D-Day at my mother's Detroit flat upset me. It wasn't about a "Hit Record" but a "Hit" on a Motown Family member by a guy who just moved into the Detroit neighborhood.

I decided I would write a manuscript about my Motown Memoirs. After all, I had been Motown's Press Officer and as its PR guy, I was always privy to all that went on behind the scenes. It was going to be a fitting response to being torpedoed.

Gordy and his no ethics and morally bankrupt hired sidekick, Michael Roshkind, did not want my Motown Memoirs to be published and wanted it destroyed or delayed.

Roshkind knowing that I supported my widowed mother preyed on my deep love for her and her well-being. He offered me the temporary delay I demanded and made me a deal that I couldn't refuse.

I flew to and from NY on airline tickets provided by Roshkind. I got to NY and I took a cab to this really dingy, scary, fuck'in office building. I walked inside and all the offices were dark. There was one office light on at the end of a very long hallway. I walked in and gave them the fake name provided to me by Roshkind.

She said, this envelope is for you. And she handed me the envelope. The only other door open was the men's room. I'm not going to fuck'in walk into the men's room and count the money and maybe get killed. I still believed it was a Roshkind setup of some kind. So, I stuck the envelope in my pocket

I finally got to another place and took a cab. I got to Broadway and went to a decent deli. I went into the bathroom there and I opened the envelope up ... Thirty, Fuck'in, Thousand Dollars. He paid me $30,000. I put it back in my pocket.

Whether Berry actually knew how Roshkind was going to temporarily block my Motown manuscript from being published is unknown as I only had direct contact with Roshkind. Roshkind told me that Berry told him to handle the matter.

Of note, I told Berry about Roshkind stealing the valor of our brave military men and women. I, also, told Berry that Roshkind had an FBI file on him. Berry ignored my concerns.

I got torpedoed and, eventually, Berry, as I stated, gave the non-valor guy a promotion to being the President of Motown.

My plane wasn't leaving from LaGuardia until the next morning. Well, I decided I was going to play it safe and kill as much time as I could.

Walking down Broadway, I heard this raspy voice yelling, Abrams... Abrams ... over here. It's James Brown wanting to pay me the $3,000 he owed me for press work I did for him. So, now I had $33,000 in cash on me. And, of course James wanted to go look for ladies of the night and wanted me to join him in this escapade. I said no. I didn't feel like getting rolled for $33,000. So, we hugged and parted ways. I headed to the airport. The airport was crawling with unsavory men. I was apprehensive and wary of contact with anyone.

I went to a pay phone to make a few calls. This is what happened and is both unbelievable and bizarre. But, it's true. I got an operator who dug my voice and kept me lingering on the phone for about an hour as she dealt with other callers and returns to me and wanted to meet me. She wanted to set up a date with me. I said no as I was leaving and hung up.

I, then, spotted two Detroit Black people I recognized. I walked with them and we got on the plane. As we were talking, she said, "Isn't this a bitch. The Detroit cab drivers went on strike."

I was not going to have a way to get from the Detroit Airport home. Here I am walking around the airport with $33,000 fuck'in dollars on me with no way to get home.

So, I call my mate, Sherry, and asked her if she could come to Detroit Metro as quick as she could to pick me up because the cab drivers are on strike. So, she came and got me.

Roshkind, then, offered a second payment to me to continue to temporarily keep my manuscript from being published. He wanted to give me $25,000. But, I later found out it wasn't for delaying the manuscript. It was for another evil and vindictive act he was orchestrating.

He stipulated these directions. I was to walk into the Hotel Ponchatrain and sit down in the lobby next to him and told not to say a fuck'in word to him. You don't know me. So, I did. I sat down next to him. All of a sudden, I felt something being shoved into my hands. He told me not to look. I grabbed it. He got up and left. I put it in my pocket and went to the bathroom. Inside was $25,000 cash.

He wanted me to help break up Holland-Dozier-Holland whom I was representing in PR. Not on my watch.

Eventually, Jimmy Hoffa's lawyer had to be hired. And, Invictus Records – Holland-Dozier-Holland went back to Motown.

Roshkind also manipulated radio DJs not to play any Mary Wells records after she departed Motown so her career would end on a low note.

Getting back to my Motown Memoirs and Roshkind. Rolling Stone wanted to run some excerpts from my manuscript. After Roshkind found out about my manuscript and a possible deal with Rolling Stone was when he said I either went along with the deal offered or told me that I had better have a real good will.

Flo Ballard was also on Roshkind's "hit list". Tommy Chapman, whom Flo married, was one of Berry's chauffers. Roshkind, basically, set up Flo with Tommy so he would get her pregnant and derail her music career. She and Tommy separated due to domestic issues and then reconciled.

Flo was a personable lady with a beautiful voice. Buttered Popcorn was a rare single featuring Flo. However, as the popularity of the record soared, Motown derailed it. It was not to get anymore airplay or promotion. Berry had already selected his Supreme Star and it was not to be Mary Wilson or Flo Ballard.

As Flo Ballard's press agent after she was forced to leave Motown was an interesting Motown twist. Flo confided in me. I respected her and only wanted to see her succeed in whatever endeavor she chose.

Having been with Berry since 1959, I saw the writing on the music wall turning from a Detroit music billboard into a Hollywood flashing billboard. Detroit's music star became a Motown footnote.

Welcome to "Hollywood".

Unpublished Motown Memoirs Manuscript 1968/1969, Al Abrams

I was Motown's Press Officer in some of America's most perilous and dangerous history moments - Civil Rights Movement, Vietnam War, Kennedy Assassination and more.

I, as Motown's front media man, created the slogans that resound with people. The Detroit Sound and Motown: The Sound of Young America. Later, I, also, had Stax-Volt labeled as The Memphis Sound.

MOTOWN MEMOIRS

Success came to me in the form of a message hastily scrawled on the back of a picture postcard.

It was a postcard from Aruba, a colorful photo showing a sunny view of a sandy beach.

I flipped the card over and looked at the azul Netherlands Antilles postage stamp with the portrait of Queen Juliana. Then I read the handwritten note.

"Dear Al: I hereby retract what I wrote in Fortune about the Supremes being unknown to most adults. By now, your P.R. job has made them as w.k. as Lyndon J.
            Sincerely, Stanley H. Brown"

I smiled at the fact that a Fortune editor would use the abbreviation for "well known" usually found in the pages of Variety. I jumped up from my desk in the publicity department of Motown Records and ran to show the card to company president Berry Gordy and anyone else I might encounter along the way. To me, the message on that card meant I had just won the Nobel Prize in Public Relations. I had hijacked Brown when I heard he was coming into Detroit to do a piece on the then-Big Four automakers and the automobile business that drove Detroit's economy.

It never seemed farfetched to me that my argument that Brown couldn't possibly tell the of 1965 Detroit without visiting Berry Gordy Jr. at the Hitsville, USA headquarters of Motown Records wasn't anything but logical. Brown must have thought so too, because he agreed, in part because he was just a short way down West Grand Boulevard at the world headquarters of General Motors, and maybe because he too was Jewish and originally from Detroit.

I gave Brown the full treatment. A long meeting with Berry. My full pitch on how the Motown Sound was changing the dynamics of American music.

"Here, say hello to America's Number One songwriting team, Holland-Dozier-Holland, they've written more hit songs than Paul McCartney and John Lennon of the Beatles."

"You've heard about Bob Dylan calling Smokey Robinson America's Greatest Living Poet. Hey, Smokey, come over here for a minute. There's someone I want you to meet."

After loading Brown up with albums, press releases, artist's photographs and multiple copies of previously published stories, he was on his way. It must have been a pleasant enough diversion; it resulted in a paragraph in his published story.

Only a paragraph? Hell yes! But what a paragraph it was It was an acknowledgment, a validation. For here in this single paragraph was Motown and Berry and the Supremes in the pages of Fortune magazine, the Bible of American capitalism.

What a breakthrough this was for blacks and a black-owned business in 1965 to even be mentioned in the same story as the presidents of GM, Ford, Chrysler and American Motors. And especially for Berry, who less than a decade ago, was himself working in a factory on an automobile assembly line. Now his name was in the same business story as the head of the company. That gave equality a new meaning.

As important as that paragraph was to Motown and my PR campaign to make every reader in the world aware of the genius of Berry Gordy, it was even more important to me. It was like a shot of adrenaline. Printed praise and mentions of Motown were my drug of choice. I was in such euphoria racing down the corridors waving the Aruba postcard like a captured enemy flag, that I literally ran into one of the white sales and promotion reps Motown hired to continue to get the airplay that fueled the fires.

Irv Biegel, whom I had worked with when he was an independent record promotion man, grabbed me and spun me around. Half-jokingly, he pulled up the sleeve of the blue short-sleeve shirt I was wearing and examined my arm. "Okay, where are those needle tracks?" he asked.

Although I was pissed off by his allusion to my being on drugs, I just smiled and kept on running. He never knew what made Al Abrams run. I had once proposed that I be allowed to wear roller skates to get down the hallways of the connected buildings in the complex to get to Berry's office quicker, but Berry had nixed the idea.

Sure, I was driven, and that's why my PR campaign and the Selling of Motown worked. It was always personal. It was my obsession. I didn't need any drugs to reach my media high skyscrapers -- MY public relations job was now recognized by a Fortune magazine editor as elevating the Supremes to the heights of President Lyndon B. Johnson.

If the last five national stories on the Supremes and Motown had been playing cards, I would have taken the jackpot. Within a few months my caption I labeled "The Detroit Sound" had broken through the public consciousness, not just in airplay and sales or network television appearances, but in the all-important area of national media coverage. And we were talking about the biggest media of that era.

The covers of Time and Newsweek. A story in Life magazine, which had sent their L.A.-based entertainment editor to Detroit. Then Look magazine and now for G-d's sake the Holy Grail, itself, Fortune magazine. It was a Grand Slam.

I also created the iconic tagline used by Motown without ever receiving the attribution and recognition that I deserve - Motown: The Sound of Young America.

I had done this all without the benefit of any formal training. I didn't have any sets of fancy initials after my name on my business cards. It was just plain Al Abrams, Director of Media Relations. My formal education ended when I graduated from high school. My real education began on my first day at Motown.

I got the job at Motown because I was lucky. On Memorial Day, 1959, I was able to get Larry Dixon, a black disc jockey on Detroit radio station WCHB, to play a record he would have ordinarily tossed in his giveaway pile.

Mike Powers -- that was his stage name -- a white Yugoslavian immigrant living across the Detroit River in Windsor, Ontario, Canada, had paid Berry and Raynoma Liles, the woman who was to become Berry's second wife, $100 to record a song called "Teenage Sweetheart.". It took me three hours of persistence to get Dixon to play the damn record just to get rid of me.

I showed up at a remote Dixon was broadcasting from, and I was determined not to leave until he played it on his show. To my knowledge, other than perhaps a radio station in his native Yugoslavia, it was the first and only time the record was ever played on the air.

Twenty-four hours earlier, I stood in the vestibule and rang the doorbell at 1719 Gladstone Avenue, the flat in Detroit where Berry. and Ray were living. There's no plaque or memorial marking the site, but that was the true birthplace of The Motown Sound.

What brought me there for that fateful meeting? Mickey Shorr, a white Jewish disk jockey at radio station WXYZ used to hold court at a popular Detroit deli. He'd always have a stack of 45's with him. The records had been given to him for airplay by promotion men, but they hadn't made the cut, and Shorr would give them away to his young fans.

One night at the deli, Shorr told my friend Sanford Freed that he could earn some extra cash by driving recording artists around to weekend record hops staged by disc jockeys. The record promoters provided the talent for free as a form of payola because they knew the disc jockey would heavily promote the record by that artist during the week before the hop.

Shorr, whose name lives on today in a Midwest-distributed line of electronic and car stereo accessories, told Freed about a black guy who had a record company and gave us his address. Freed didn't want to go into the inner city by himself, so I said I'd gladly accompany him.

During my first meeting with Berry, I concentrated upon two things. The music he played for us on his stereo (He gave me that stereo as a Christmas gift that year.) and the chili in a pot being stirred by the woman taking care of a young child in the house.

Freed wasn't impressed but I was intrigued by the music, overpowered by the smell of chili and taken in by the charismatic couple with a fledgling music company.

But Berry wasn't too taken with me. He handed me a record and said, "if you can get this played, I'll hire you". After I left, I later learned that he told Raynoma "You can bet I'll never see that white boy again."

The record was on the Zelman label. Berry later told me he chose that name because it sounded Jewish, the same logic he had employed for his Stein and Van Stock Music Publishing Company.

I was on a mission. Unbeknownst to me, Berry and Raynoma were driving on Belle Isle, the popular near-downtown Detroit park on Memorial Day, and listening to WCHB when "Teenage Sweetheart" came on the air. Raynoma later told me that Berry almost lost control of the car and drove into the river. "I can't believe it," he told her. "That white boy got the record played. Now I have to hire him."

That's exactly what Berry did when I showed up on his doorstep again the next day. He was always a tough bargainer but we struck a good deal. I'd come to work for the Rayber Music Company (named after both RAYnoma and BERry) for $25 a week and all the chili I could eat.

And yes, I had to drive artists to record hops on the weekends. That became real fun whenever a sudden rainstorm developed and I couldn't get my convertible top up, and I delivered a sopping wet Eddie Holland or Marv Johnson to a record hop.

Berry looked at me as if I were a genius and asked what was I going to do next.

Well, I had just had a record played on the air for the first time, so why not go for broke?

So, I went to Windsor and met the man now known as Mike Powers, who technically should hold the title in the Guinness Book of World Records of being the world's first Motown recording artist.

I took Powers to the entertainment editor of his adopted hometown's daily newspaper, The Windsor Star. There, he was interviewed and photographed wearing his Frank Sinatra-look-alike straw hat, as unlikely a teenage singing idol as you'll ever see, and I now became a press agent. Me – a Jewish white kid – now a real teenage press agent for a Black-owned record company.

I remembered what I had seen Tony Curtis do in one of my favorite movies The Sweet Smell of Success in which he had played a press agent. So, I talked lots of drivel about a fan club and legions of fans. Although I must have come across as a combination of a carnival broker and P.T. Barnum, they ran the story the next day, and I took the tunnel bus across the river to buy copies. I used to fish the story out of the Star library 25 years later when that paper hired me as a reporter, a job I'd always craved.

But what do I do for Berry as an encore? Eddie Holland, Marv Johnson and Smokey Robinson were some of the talented singers who were already in Berry's stable. I wrote hyped-up biographies for them and then dealt with another dilemma.

As their records were released, they had the opportunity to appear on Detroit Bandstand, a local television show where they could lip synch their songs. But they didn't have proper stage outfits.

I had a plan. There was a store called Hot Sam's in downtown Detroit that sold shirts and vests with glitter and other gaudy stage performer clothes that I used to buy and wear. I once showed up in one of those sparkly outfits at the home of a prominent Jewish Detroit financier whose daughter I was taking out on a date. He answered the door, took one look at me and slammed the door in my face.

Today, it would be the equivalent of my showing up in hooded hip-hop gear with numerous body tats and weighted down by twenty pounds of gold medallions and chains. It's called first impressions. Fortunately, he never associated me with the specter at his door when I profiled him for business stories years later.

I went to see the owners of Hot Sam's and made them a proposition they could not turn down.

If Hot Sam's would outfit each of our stars, we'd give the store a plug on Detroit Bandstand. They agreed to try it first with Eddie Holland. I made sure Eddie got the plug in when Dale Young, the host of the show interviewed him. The next two were easy.

How different is this from today's NASCAR drivers literally covered head-to-toe in sponsorship stickers? I was really writing a how-to promotional and branding manual for the marketing industry without even knowing it.

And if there was already such a manual available, I didn't know about it. I was winging it every minute 24/7.

I was fortunate in that I had already met some of Detroit's black disc jockeys when, at the age of 14, I took a streetcar to downtown Detroit and the offices of the Detroit Tribune, a black weekly newspaper. I asked the editor if I could write a weekly gossip column for Central High School that I wanted to call the Central Chatterbox. They agreed and on Oct. 24, 1955 gave me my first byline.

After I graduated from Central in January 1957, I kept the column alive by turning it into a weekly-Top Ten records listings reporting what was being played most frequently by a rotation of disc jockeys on WJLB, then the only black-oriented radio station in the city. Every week I'd pick up the listings from Joltin' Joe Howard, Frantic Ernie Durham, Long Tall Lean, Lanky Larry Dean and Senator Bristoe Bryant and turn the song lists into a readable column long before radio stations began to print and handout their own airplay lists. Yes. I was following my passion for music. Politics, books, journalism and social issues completed my personal passion list.

Music is not neutral. It is an emotional rollercoaster that draws in millions of fans. Artists do bring their personal baggage, political agendas and social platforms to the stage as they evolve into mega-stars. So, it made sense to me that my other notable passions aligned with selling music. It still makes sense today.

Those early contacts made it much easier for me to approach the WJLB disc jockeys as a promotion man for Motown, or more accurately Jobete, Berry's music publishing arm.

For me, it was continuing my love affair with rhythm and blues music that began when I was still in high school and used to lay under the covers of my bed with my transistor radio listening to Hoss Allen and John R., the disc jockeys on WLAC Radio in Nashville, Tennessee which I could pick up on a clear signal after ten p.m.

I never dreamed that within three years I'd be meeting them personally at a national rhythm and blues disk jockey convention in a hotel on the Atlantic City boardwalk, much less asking them to spin Motown records on their shows for me.

I was also a pioneer music groupie of sorts. When the Shirelles played a date in Detroit, I found the name of the motel at which they were staying in Highland Park and showed up after the show in full glitter and tried unsuccessfully to get a date with any or all of them. The "Sweet Smell of Success"- not.

Detroit always attracted a huge number of recording artists who appeared on television shows like the 11 p.m. Soupy Sales show on WXYZ-TV. As a "reporter" from the Detroit Tribune complete with a homemade press card, I would show up backstage for the chance to meet and talk with the black artists like the Platters, once totally ignoring a young Paul Newman on his first Hollywood promotional tour. Go figure.

I used to go to Hastings Street in Detroit's Black Bottom to hang out at the recordshop owned and operated by blues legend John Lee Hooker and buy 78's by artists like the Crows, the Falcons (You're So Fine) and the Royal Jokers (a half-century later, I can still sing the lyrics to You Tickle Me Baby), records that you couldn't find elsewhere. I'd walk to and from black neighborhoods, carrying my fragile 78's and never encountered any problems. By the time I went to work for Motown, I was accustomed to being the only white face in an all-black milieu.

After I graduated, I lied about my age and was hired by the Handleman Company, the pioneer mass music distributor. I worked in the pre-computer order tracking division. It was a job I wanted because Handleman gave their employees a discount on buying new records, and that was where the rest of my salary went when I wasn't buying glitter fashion. Although I certainly can't claim any credit for it, the Handleman Company grew despite their hiring me – an underage employee. Eventually, Handleman became an industry giant. whose financial successes I would frequently chronicle 40 years later as a business reporter.

Who could've guessed that Handleman's then CEO Steven Strome would be the big brother of my high school best friend, Marshall, and that the latter would make his own brand of history by becoming the first person to successfully perform a larynx transplant -- another event I would cover as a reporter.

There was one sure-fire way to market a record in 1959 and that was payola.

After Joltin' Joe Howard left WJLB for WCHB, I would drive out to their studios in Inkster, Michigan, stopping to buy an expensive bottle of Cutty Sark on my way.

Although I wasn't legally old enough to buy alcohol, no one ever asked for my ID.

When I got to the station, I said hello to the beautiful and friendly receptionist Elsie Frazier, with whom Berry later had a longtime affair. I frequently played sentry at the front desk of Hitsville (Berry and Ray lived upstairs over the studio) to tip Berry off if Ray returned home early from a Saturday morning shopping trip. Cast in that unwelcome, divisive and morally-bankrupt role, I felt like one of the White House guards who the music business rumor mill reported were doing much the same for President John Kennedy. I was young, stupid and wanted to keep my job.

At the station, I walked into the glassed-in broadcast studio where Howard was on the air, gave him the bottle and often slipped him another ten dollars before putting the record I was carrying on his turntable to be the next disk he aired. I knew Berry was anxiously listening at Hitsville to hear how the record sounded on the radio.

I later learned that instead of spending three hours in the sun at Larry Dixon's Memorial Day remote, I could have accomplished the same goal much earlier by giving him a return airline ticket for a flight to New York -- or an introduction to one of my many stone foxes. Never, ever did I exchange drugs for airplay, a practice that became even more prevalent after I moved from promotions to Motown's press officer at the tender age of 18.

The record industry is a competitive cutthroat industry where selling the music and the artists is an exchange system of hip-hop and rap music

"I remember all too well those days of payola," recalls Ofield Dukes, who served as WCHB's first news director from 1958 to 1961. Dukes later became administrative assistant to Vice President Hubert H. Humphrey and was instrumental in the creation of the "Stay in School" campaign, which I used to help catapult Otis Redding and the Memphis Sound to worldwide fame after I'd left Motown.

Don't get me started about payola as a sales tool. I always thought it had another side when it came to black disk jockeys working on black-oriented radio stations.

Everyone knew they weren't being paid anywhere near what their white counterparts were receiving. The radio station owners knew it and turned a blind eye to the practice.

After Barrett Strong recorded the anthem "Money, That's What I Want" for Berry's sister Anna's label, we spent hours deciding how to debut what we instinctively knew could be one of Berry's most commercial productions. The decision? I would fly to New York a few days before Christmas with a dub, the oversize acetate of the song, and give $100 to Alan Freed, the legendary disk jockey who created the term "Rock 'n' Roll" and let him "break" the song over WABC radio.

The irony of giving Freed $100 in payola to then spin a record called "Money, That's What I Want" at a time when payola investigations were already being rumored was not lost upon me as I took a cab from the airport to WABC's studios.

Once there, I took my place on a long series of wooden benches outside the studio, populated by other record promotion men all with records (and presumably cash plus incentives) in hand.

I was thrilled to meet Freed when my name was called and we talked during the time a record was on the air. He listened to "Money" first, then I gave him the real money and sat outside the studio as he spun the disk. I thought he was truly sincere in his praise and enthusiasm for the song, and it came across that way to his listeners.

When I left the studio, I flagged down a cab and asked the white driver to take me to the Hotel Theresa in Harlem.

Because we had little money to spend, Berry, Ray and I had earlier shared a room at the Theresa on my first trip to New York. We came to Manhattan to meet with United Artists, the label that leased the first Marv Johnson recordings. We flipped a coin and I slept on the floor and Berry and Ray shared the bed. I never told them I had won the bed in the coin toss. Berry and Ray were not only my bosses but my friends.

However, this time the cab driver refused and said no one would risk driving me uptown to 125th Street and Seventh Avenue at that time of night. I walked ... all the way to Harlem stopping to listen to music playing inside Black-owned bars.

Would I do anything to get airplay on a white radio station? Chuck Daugherty hosted the all-night show on WXYZ which meant he had some leeway in slipping in a song or two not yet on the station's approved playlist. When Daugherty had to move to a new house, he asked if I knew anyone who could help him. I told Berry and the instant moving team of Holland-Dozier-Holland was born.

Yes, the same Holland-Dozier-Holland team of songwriters who would write the song hits that put the Supremes on the map. But on this Saturday morning, they were my crew of workers assisting a DJ on the move.

When we decided to take a break, the five of us walked into a bar in Farmington, Michigan on Eight Mile Road, the main artery later immortalized by rapper Eminem in his movie "8 Mile".

We ordered hamburgers and Cokes but the bar owner wouldn't serve Eddie Holland, his brother Brian, or Lamont Dozier and told them they had to leave. However, he said the two white guys who came in with them could stay.

We all agreed that was not the time and place to make a stand, so we bought burgers in a bag and sat in the bar's parking lot eating them. Today, Holland-Dozier-Holland could probably buy that entire block in Farmington with the pocket change from their royalties.

Before I realized that the way to get a record played often meant having a little black book that was the best in town, and one that wasn't just restricted to phone numbers of attractive members of the opposite sex, I thought I'd found the answer in staging theatrical promotional stunts. It was something that I'd read about in the biographies of legendary press agents and decided to apply to Motown.

My motive was to get photographs of the stunts into national publications, just like the legendary movie company press agents had done in the past. The amazing thing is that it worked, mainly because no one else in the record promotion business felt the need to dress up in outlandish costumes when an envelope full of cash could accomplish the same result.

On a cold morning in Detroit, I was out at the crack of dawn wearing one of my mother's old bed sheets pulling off another publicity stunt just to get a Motown record played on the local airwaves. I was too young to realize the irony of an 18-year-old Jewish kid promoting a record by black artists on a black-owned label while wearing the symbol of the KKK's racial oppression. But I wasn't playing this by any Public Relations 101 text book. They didn't teach PR in the high school I had graduated from at 15.

Maybe that was the secret of my success. I was always too dumb to know all the possible ramifications of what I was really doing.

Fortunately, I had some other costume props to go along with the king-sized sheet. I was wearing a turban and a fake beard. And I was carrying a long rubber snake that looked like a phallic symbol, especially when Detroit's top DJ, Tom Clay of WJBK, was photographed deep-throating it. The photograph of me in the costume next to Berry holding the snake with a fabulous startled look on his face is almost an icon of early Motown.

I commandeered Berry's Pontiac Bonneville convertible, affixed two hand-made primitive posters to the side of each door, and with my personal photographer in tow was off to make the world aware of a record called "Snakewalk" by an instrumental group comprised of Motown studio musicians named for the occasion as the "The Swinging Tigers."

Maybe I liked that record and chose to promote it because it reminded me of an instrumental I had cut in my mother's living room earlier that year and gone to Chicago with Sanford Freed to try to sell the song to Leonard and Phil Chess of Chess Records.

On the way to Chicago, I was pulled over for speeding by the Ohio State Highway Patrol in Wauseon, Ohio. I only avoided arrest and missing my meeting at Chess because the trooper admired my watch which wound up on his wrist. Once again, there was serendipity at play.

I do have enormous respect for law enforcement patrols that place themselves at risk for public safety. Unfortunately, it happened. And we made it to Chicago.

Chess Records was one of the first record companies I had dealt with in leasing one of Berry's compositions. I was already familiar with the turf.

Despite getting the photos of the disk jockeys looking foolish into the music business trades -- which went a long way to establishing the Motown name in the minds of industry insiders -- and the local airplay that the stunt generated, Snakewalk was a huge disappointment. It was the last time I'd try a wild stunt to get Motown publicity – for at least five years.

I quickly realized there were other ways to keep Tamla and Motown's name on the national publicity front. I set up an informal job service program for out of work disk jockeys which consisted of notifying the trade publications -- Billboard, the aptly named Cashbox and Record World -- along with their contact information. Every time I reported on the comings and goings of the DJ's to the music trades, I automatically got another plug-in for the Motown name. Not only was running a job search with good results a way to sell Motown, it earned me a cascade of IOU's from more disk jockeys who would be eager to spin my records.

In fact, I had labels printed up reading "Thanks for the spin - Al Abrams" which I always affixed to the "A" side of a record. I also printed a supply of post cards at the Gordy Printing Company owned by one of Berry's brothers. These cards promoted the "Al Abrams Top Pick" which, of course, was the record I was working on getting played that week.

I handed those out everywhere as if they were political campaign flyers -- which in some aspects they were. While my job was the branding of Motown, I wasn't ignoring the value of my name.

I also created the first print ads for Jobete and Motown songs for the trades. My first impression of the trades was that they earned that name because record companies traded full page ads for favorable reviews.

Sometimes I was forced to make my own news when it came to my DJ employment service. There's been a lot of speculation over the years about how Detroit DJ Lee Alan was fired from his job at WJBK on charges that he accepted payola. That was the first time payola charges had been brought against a Motor City air personality, and Alan's firing made the front pages of the Detroit dailies.

The reality was that I trumped up the charges against Alan. Why? Simply because when I asked him why he wasn't playing Motown recordings the way other DJ's at the station were doing, he made a racist crack about blacks and black men trying to become record moguls.

I went back to my office in the Hitsville attic and drafted a telegram by hand on a sheet of yellow legal paper. I addressed it to George Storer, the head of Storer

Broadcasting, the company that owned WJBK. I knew he wouldn't give a crap about Alan's racist comments, so I suggested Storer investigate Alan for payola. I signed the telegram with the fictional name Coalition of Concerned Citizens and threatened to use all our combined force to call for an FCC investigation and a boycott of the station if Storer did not take immediate action.

I sent the telegram from a pay phone at the Cunningham's Drug Store down the street from Hitsville while Berry sat at the lunch counter. He had no idea of what I was doing. The next day, Alan was fired. The moral of the lesson was Don't Fuck with Motown, especially if you're a bigot.

Was Alan actually on the take? I didn't know for sure, but I figured if he was, his bosses would quickly find out. Fortunately for me, no one at Storer thought of tracing the telegram sent via Western Union.

Berry believed in me and that's what counted. After all, I was his national promotion director, the person solely in charge of getting every disto play Motown records. And by God, I was going to do it overnight.

That chance came quick enough. Badgering the Detroit Times, the Hearst daily that was then one of Detroit's three daily newspapers, for a newspaper story was really nothing new for me.

When I was ten, I used to take the streetcars downtown every Saturday and annoy the editors until they gave me goodies like Spanish-American war issues to take home just to get rid of me. I won a ribbon in a 1953 statewide Search Grandma's Attic contest with one of those issues.

Years later, as Motown's PR director, more than one editor looked in my eyes and said "You look familiar kid, have we met somewhere before?"

The payoff came in the form of a Detroit Times story by Jerry Kabel, who later served as press secretary to Michigan's great liberal senator Philip A. Hart. The Senate office building in Washington is named in Hart's honor.

The column marked the first appearance by Berry and Smokey in a daily, as well as for "Al Abrams, the studio's promotion director." Kabel's column covered the city. I never foresaw I'd be writing a similar column for another metropolitan daily 40 years later.

Kabel's column was called "Detroit: Three Million Stories," and it appeared in the lower corner of the Times' back page. Kabel described Berry as "president of a recording studio at 2648 W. Grand that he believes is the only one in Detroit devoted to popular music rather than singing commercials."

Berry is quoted as saying "Songs are composed, arranged and master-recorded right in this building."

That's when Al Abrams, the studio's promotion man, makes his debut with his spiel. Kabel paraphrased it as "Hundreds of aspiring artists crowd Gordy's studio every month, certain that they have the necessary voice talent for overnight (success).

Rather than turn them rudely away, the studio has arranged a coaching and music promising singers under contract."

Then I moved in for the kill.

As Kabel explained, "The best thing we've got going right now is 'You Got What it Takes' by Marv Johnson, said Mr. Abrams, searching my face for some sign of recognition. Disappointed, he pointed out reprovingly, 'It reached fifth place in the national popularity ratings.' He searched out a recording of the song, put it on a turntable and Johnson's voice throbbed ..."

When the story ran the day after the interview, I convinced Berry of its (and my) worth by telling him to consider it a free ad. "What would this have cost us? We could never have afforded it," I told him. Not only were we selling the $100 program, but we had free promotion for our artists and our songs in a newspaper read by white folks.

Soon I followed that triumph with an even bigger success -- getting Motown into the hallowed pages of Jet magazine.

The Miracles had been booked to do a show in St. Louis for black disk jockey Dave Dixon. I shared part of the drive as our Volkswagen bus went through endless stretches of Indiana and Illinois farmland before crossing the Mississippi River.

I celebrated that event by parking the bus in front of the first used book store I saw to indulge my whim for collecting old magazines. I ran inside and spent about 15 minutes poring over old National Geographic magazines while the bookstore owner and his employees peered nervously out the picture window at the busload of restless blacks wearing doo-rags parked in front of their store.

The Miracles show was what we called a smash. So many fans turned out to see and hear Smokey, Claudette and the group that police had to be called to keep order.

Bells went off in my head to match the sirens I was hearing. Here was a news story I didn't have to make up -- maybe only exaggerate a little. I called Berry and got the home phone number of Chester Higgins, an editor at Jet magazine in Chicago. Higgins, the father of award-winning photographer Chester Higgins, Jr., had worked on the Michigan Chronicle, the Detroit black weekly.

Jet was the popular digest sized news and entertainment weekly published by Johnson Publications along with Ebony. Of course, by the time I gave Higgins the story, the incident had somewhat gravitated into a full-scale riot by Smokey's fans. Using Berry's expensive Leicaflex, an expensive 35mm German camera, (which later became yet another of his Christmas gifts to me), I shot some photos of the crowd scene.

I remember the look on Berry's face when we waited at Cunningham's for the copies of the following week's Jet to be put on the magazine rack. With one stroke of luck I had made a major breakthrough for the Miracles and Motown in the national black media.

Jet was then the most widely read black publication in the nation. The home of news about the black recording superstars like Sam Cooke and Dinah Washington, it opened the doors for the Pittsburgh Courier, Afro-American newspapers and Chicago Defender chains to get on my Motown bandwagon. The St. Louis "riot" became part of Motown folklore. It wasn't the first time that my PR was to play that role.

Finally, I had a viable game plan. Build Motown nationally first through the black media and locally with both white and black media.

I knew I could sell Motown to the world the way I had sold myself to Berry, even if I had to invent my empire. And soon enough, I had my chance.

Berry had created a new label he named Miracle. I had opposed the name and trained a phone receptionist to answer all incoming calls on that line with the greeting, "Good morning. If it's a hit, it's a Miracle."

I don't think anyone ever caught on.

However, soon enough, the Miracle label went from bearing the brunt of my practical jokes to becoming one of my most important tools in the selling of Motown.

Joel Sebastian held down the pivotal 7 p.m. to midnight slot on WXYZ. I really liked Joel as a person, and when he let the information slip to me one day that he had always wanted to cut a record, I went into high gear.

The result was that Joel Sebastian became a Miracle recording artist. So what if he was the only one playing his song, he was soon giving lots of other Motown records exposure, not just in Detroit, but later at WLS in Chicago where he became the station's top disk jockey before tragically dying of natural causes. Had he lived, there is no doubt in my mind that he would have gone on to a career in television.

And when I found out that a well known Chicago disc jockey who did have a television show also had a protégé who was an aspiring country and western singer, Debbie Dean soon made her Miracle debut.

Years later, I would ghostwrite album liner notes which would be published under the names of television and radio personalities we needed to reach. But perhaps the ultimate coup was having Marvin Gaye, at the peak of his career, record a record and commercial for the Detroit Free Press when they launched their Teen Page.

Slowly but surely, I was turning the selling of Motown into an art form.

My Motown years helped Berry to imagine and create a global music record label while promoting the label's artists. What I didn't deserve is how Motown decided I was no longer to be part of "The Family".

Hitsville's Attic Office

Al Abrams Teenage Motown Boy

Al Abrams Motown Man

Al & Berry

Al Abrams Explains His
Motown Memoirs Unpublished Manuscript

Jerry Cavanagh was the Mayor of Detroit. He was on the cover of Look magazine. People were boosting him as the success story. He could be the governor; wind up as a presidential candidate. And George Romney, who later wound up in Nixon's cabinet; Romney was governor of Michigan. Romney would show up at the Michigan State Fair when the Supremes were there, go on stage with them and introduce them. Governor Jennifer Granholm would do the same back in the sixties, you just had that reaching out, that link, just to be able to touch and be a part of that Motown phenomenon—it was just something unheard of for the city.

I mean sure, the city had sports heroes, the city certainly had Joe Louis, but this was nothing like it; there was just nothing like it. It was a phenomenon. I don't even think Eminem and 8-Mile even comes close to it. It was just far more wide-ranging than that. But a lot of it has to do with timing. A lot of it has to do with the Beatles, with the Dave Clark 5, with the Rolling Stones acknowledging their discovery of Motown long before white Americans did - a lot of serendipity. Take a look in my archive and see if you can get a hold of Berry's book "To Be Loved". Take a look and see what Berry has to say on that.

I believed it was important to have the political connections to enable Motown and its artists to interact and solidify relationships to present a unified message to the music industry about America's dance floors and concert stages.

Personal Interview with Al Abrams - Unpublished Motown Manuscript

*On his friendship with Berry Gordy…

Berry even learned Yiddish, just to communicate with my mother. Berry and I were like brothers — we wore each other's clothes. I can't believe there was a time I could wear Berry Gordy's clothes. We just had a lot of fun together.

There were these Korean singers called the Kim Sisters—a couple of foxes. We tried to pick them up at the airport. Berry decided our best strategy was to have him pretend to be my valet. Pretend that I was a high society guy. But we couldn't pick them up.

In Washington, D.C. when Ben-Hur came out — at that time the Washington theatres were segregated — I knew about the African diplomat exemption — so Berry spoke African gibberish at the box office. I explained that he was an African diplomat, and we got to sit together.

*You mention in your Memoir manuscript that Detroit and Motown became almost synonymous. What led to Motown becoming identified with Detroit?

I think the help of the media, especially television ... TV shows, the disc jockeys, the Free Press and eventually the Detroit News. It's just unparalleled; you just don't see anything like that anymore, where everyone's playing a part in it. Everybody wanted to have a piece of it, basically.

*So Motown became identified with Detroit because everyone in Detroit wanted to get in on the Motown phenomenon?

Oh I think so, yes, because it was something to be proud of. There was a lot of pride for the city. You have to remember - Detroit's pretty gritty city scape.

*To what extent did Motown want to be identified with Detroit?

I remember some of the reluctance about putting the map of Detroit on the Motown label — there was some real worry that it might backfire — but that warmness and that acceptance meant a lot - it helped create a family feeling.

*Did this desire for identification or lack thereof change over time?

That would carry over more into other aspects—when the Marvelettes did "Please Mr. Postman" — we didn't put a picture of the group on the cover. We didn't want to over-promote their blackness. We figured everybody knew about it. But just the same, when Berry Gordy's brother Bob recorded, they changed his name to Bob Kayli. They tried to get into the white market without letting everyone know they were black. Particularly, we were worried that some of the Southern white disc jockeys might not play the records and the record stores wouldn't sell them. But that turned out to be unfounded — once the breakthrough came, it came. This was before "branding."

*In the draft for your Motown Memoirs that you produced in late 60's you claim that "Motown betrayed Detroit." Could you talk a little bit about what you meant by that — what form did Motown's betrayal take?

Motown ultimately betrayed Detroit] by leaving it. I think the decision to move Motown to LA was not a wise one. Going ahead and making it a coastal entity tied directly into motion pictures left behind a lot of "Motown Family". Could have stayed here and opened a branch in LA. That's when the honeymoon ended — the media really took Motown to task for this.

*What effect do you think Motown's leaving Detroit had on the attitudes of the people and the press of Detroit toward the company?

It saddened everybody as a lot of people felt betrayed. They felt that they were sold out. They'd put a lot into Motown where Motown became a part of their lives and then Motown turned their back on them. It was like losing a lover, as I indicated in a couple of bitter chapters [in my memoir manuscript] you've had access to.

*And, as a result of this, do you know what happened to Motown's popularity, in Detroit and abroad?

It waned, it certainly waned — it was a boon for me, because by this time I was working for Stax/Volt, I named The Memphis Sound. And it made it even more possible for me to create the alternative, and in some cases even, in the minds of many people, the replacement for Motown as another pop phenomenon.

It's really interesting because there's a movie out today called Hustle and Flow that is set in Memphis, although it's rap oriented. I think the Free Press and News this morning made the parallels to Eminem's 8-Mile story, so you still have that little classic struggle between Detroit and Memphis in terms of music.

I started to question: am I able to get these incredible results, to do this because of the product that I'm working with — or could I do it with something else? So when the opportunity came to do it somewhere else, I jumped.

*Motown is often thought of as "crossover" music. Indeed, the company was able to market effectively to whites — one of the first instances of white audiences listening to black artists. How did the company create this crossover? What measures were taken to attract white listeners, and what effect do you think they had?

I don't know if anyone has ever truly figured out how it happened. But in town, we were being played by all the white stations. More and more white people became cognizant of the music. One of the things Berry did — you'd play it on a really tinny phonograph — recreate the radio sound—and if it still sounded good, it was a go. The timing was just perfect. The Beatles had said some really complementary things. British groups talked about the influence of the Motown sound.

*How about marketing to African-Americans? How did the way Motown pitched itself to blacks differ from the way it pitched itself to whites—and did one racial constituency come first?

Basically, I don't think there were any differences. I drew no distinctions—and I don't think any distinction was ever drawn. Most of the people handling national promotion were white and would steer exclusively toward white radio stations. We didn't play the game of denying access to black media, but then again that was during my regime; once I left, things changed. The concentration on black media changed. At Stax Records, I would hear a lot of complaints from the black press about how the new regime at Motown wasn't cooperating with them.

I don't want that to sound self-serving, but I had my own style, and it was certainly replaced with a more polished style that you would buy from the big-time L.A. publicity firms. Barbara Holliday, a good friend and a writer for the Freep, once said my press releases, which she said flooded the media with every detail of Motown's life, were written in a "Baroque" style, and she probably was right.

*You talk in your memoir manuscript about "Motown's bourgeois" who were "so anxious to become white that the black community tagged them "Oreos" – black on the outside and white within." How did this thirst for whiteness manifest itself and what do you think caused it?

There was an association — with money, all things change. Some people who had long term relationships with black females or black males dumped the blacks for whites. There are times when a blond is a status symbol in the black community, just check out a rap video. Moving out of the ghetto and moving into white neighborhoods became that type of status. And it's funny, here I am, and I'm trying to emulate blacks (I had a Jew-Fro) and I'm seeing these black people trying to emulate whites.

*How "true to their roots" were the Motown artists, both in terms of their music —the kind of music they produced — and

socially, as in the way they acted, they way they behaved? And were some artists and even some executives "truer" than others? And did they try to give back to the community?

Oh yes, we always gave back to the community. A lot of free appearances—a lot of things we just never talked about because we didn't do it for the publicity. Motown and especially Berry helped a lot of people. There were a lot of generous people, very generous people there. They were always ready to help friends, trying to help pull up a lot of friends. Again, family is the word it has to come back to – Motown Family was my standard as the Press Officer.

True to their roots? Yeah - during my tenure. In terms of the executives, some of the people who came on later, who didn't work their way up through the program, the later hires to run departments as the company got bigger, you wouldn't expect them to have the same "family" philosophy… and they didn't.

*Which was? That first philosophy was?

There's a song — we used to start meetings off with a song called Hitsville U.S.A. The first lines are "We are a very swinging company here at Hitsville, U.S.A." We actually, used to start off the meetings singing this song. Some of the Motown books, I know, some people have reprinted the entire lyrics. I could never get them straight then, and I still can't get them straight now. But Berry would – always. If Berry thought that you were faking the lyrics, he'd choose you to lead the song. That would always be oops, embarrassing time. But yeah, you got a company that starts out with that, keeps the meanings like that. It's not your Harvard Business School way of running the company.

*Thinking about issues of race, did you notice, or did any artists talk to you about, a difference for them—as black artists—working for a black-owned company rather than a white owned company? How did—do you know, at all, how the treatment they received differed, if it did at all?

Boy, you're going to have to really find one of the artists, or someone black. I'd be out of line answering that. We didn't have a whole lot of time for philosophical discussions.

I don't think we ever thought that what we were doing was making history. It was just—we were in there every day and every night, and we were working, and having a lot of fun. A lot of those issues — if they were dealt with — I wasn't privy to them, probably with good reason. There were no outbursts of hostility, there was no racial tension. It just didn't exist. Did not exist at all while I was there.

Let me give you one story: Coming back from Cleveland — it was the night that Berry and I and a couple of other people wrote Marv Johnson's "I Love the Way You Love". When we were passing through the Detroit-Windsor tunnel, coming back into the States, and the customs officer on the U.S. side, asked the guys up front who they were (I think John Oden was driving) and he then looked in the back. I was sitting in back with Berry and Robert Bateman, and he said, "And who do we have here in the back?" Berry said, "ain't nobody in back here but us niggers." And the guy said "UHH", kinda' looked real funny and then he walked away. But then he came back and he shined his light on me [laughs], and he looked for a minute and thought "wait a minute, did I hear that right?" But then he didn't push it, he just walked away. So, if you take that in the right spirit, I think you know what I'm saying.

*Indeed, how did Motown work with its stars? How were they discovered, and how were they signed? What steps were taken to market them—from the famous "charm school" to your press releases?

The Motown Machine — that's what the Free Press tagged it. My take on it: Motown cared about the artists — Motown went all out for its artists, and the artists went all out for Motown. Everyone was pretty much family.

*Motown was called a "hit machine," and you were talking, of course, about writing a song… To you, as someone who helped write and publicize and get these songs played, how did this

machine work from the writing to the airplay and who and what made it so reliable?

I didn't get involved in song writing again — that was a one-time fluke and I couldn't recreate it. So that was it. I never wrote another hit song again, or another song that would even make it past anyone's consideration. So, that's a fluke. But in terms of product — I'd hear the product — I'd hear it after a recording session and I'd hear it in the studio. I'd just hear it and I'd just get so caught up in it, and just go "Aww, Man"!

I just couldn't wait to get my hands on it and get out there and promote it. During '59/'60 I was more involved in getting airplay. By the mid-sixties - Motown's getting media attention and newspaper coverage. So, between the two lines — there's a clear demarcation. I'm no longer involved in airplay from probably '63 on, that's all handled by the sales and promotions staff. I'm the P.R. arm of the Motown Machine. I am Motown's press/media guy.

*On the writing side?

You can't leave anybody out of it. It was pretty hard work. Norm Whitfield, Smokey Robinson, Janie Bradford, Barrett Strong, Robert Bateman. People really worked hard at the business of writing songs, and people worked hard at the business of music — we had quality control meetings. Berry took that from the Ford Motor Company. Something would not get out — people would vote on it. People would make side bets. A lot of it never got out. Once we knew that the record was going to be out, that's when all the elements went into play.

We didn't realize we were doing this. We were creating legends? We didn't have time to think of that.

*You write about Berry Gordy's media image. What was it?

Berry was accessible and would always honestly answer reporters' questions. Berry didn't hide. He was always there; he was always available. The image wasn't hyped. Berry conveyed it himself, that whole spirit of openness. The Free Press made Detroit readers a part of the Motown family. If you called me in 1964 and you were doing what you are trying to do today — you'd wind up with some face-to-face time with Berry Gordy. Maybe not a lot, but maybe he'd take a liking to you.

*One way music listeners choose their likes and dislikes is by seeking out "authentic" material—material that they see as "real music"—music that is original, artistic, and composed and played from the heart and soul—as opposed to some spinoff or imitation. What, to you, defines "authentic music"?

I'm really not qualified to answer. In the early days, on Sunday nights, Berry, Raynoma and I would go around to the black churches and we'd listen to the spirituals. Many of those songs would wind up in Motown — you just take "Oh Lord" or "Oh Jesus" and replace it with "Oh Baby" — but still that doesn't mean that the final Motown creation wasn't original.

*You mention that the Beatles looked at Motown as representative of African-American music. What do you think of the authenticity of Motown music and do you think that the American public saw it as authentic? Were some Motown stars more or less "authentic" than others?

See, white kids in England picked up quicker than white kids in the U.S. on Motown. And the Brits had a lot of tabloids that covered the news that had a lot of influence. They had a Tamla-Motown Appreciation Society and came to visit us. I think that the original crest may have spilled over — that may have contributed to that acceptance by white teenagers of the product — this stuff was so good, you couldn't ignore it. It just dominated the airways. If you look at a movie on TV about the '60's or '70's that's Motown on the soundtrack. Motown displaced the Beatles. Holland-Dozier-Holland wrote more hit records than Lennon and McCartney.

The Reverend Martin Luther King, Jr. was a Motown "artist" — The "I Have a Dream" speech was recorded by Motown. Martin Luther King Jr. who actually had a Motown recording contract.

By '64, Berry started finding artists, people that he grew up liking that in a lot of cases needed recording contracts that no one else would give them. We even tried to sign one of Lyndon Johnson's daughters — that was some of my great PR hype for white audiences. We were signing people for PR purposes — and that ultimately set the foundation for the move to the west. There was probably a link to it, when you start picking up Las Vegas-type acts like "Billy Eckstine, Tony Martin, Bobby Breen, Jack Soo, the Asian-American actor on the show "Barney Miller," just people, lounge acts — not Motown artists but people who had name recognition. It was like, "Oh boy, look, we signed them to Motown now and they're coming here now". In retrospect, it was an error as we never had a big hit with any of them. But media-wise, in terms of publicity, you milk it like crazy. You know, they're coming to you at Motown now because you're the hottest record label around.

*How did this begin, and how did it lead to the departure?

Berry would meet these — I don't want to say down-on-their-luck artists because they probably had a lot more money than we ever knew but these artists wanted to connect with a big music company. Berry had a hard time saying no to people. But these were people with extraordinary talent and great reputations; I just don't think they were the right mix. They weren't going to get their careers revitalized with a Holland-Dozier-Holland son — it just didn't happen. It just started to get us away from where the Detroit family roots were and where the dynamics were. It went too far pop — or to be more, blunt, it went too far white - sort of the whitening of Motown. But it's okay for me to say that, because I'm white.

*Closely tied to the notion of authenticity is that of musical genre. What genres did Motown bill itself as producing and were these genre labels fair? Which artists filled which genre slots?

I came up with the "Sound of Young America" — that was basically it. A little bit of everything.

We were trying to open those doors to get the classier bookings. Get them off the Chitlin' Circuit — the black entertainment circuit ... any record company wants to do that – expand.

[On post-L.A. move authenticity] Motown lost its soul. There was a decline in its public popularity — which was beneficial for me. Stax Volt, the sound of Memphis, supplanted it as the more authentic black sound. You get more pop into the songs at Motown. It wasn't authentic any longer, with some exceptions like Marvin Gaye. The public can always tell what's real and what's not.

*How did Motown try to open doors to classier bookings for its artists — get them off the "Chitlin' Circuit"?

By recording the Supremes on albums designed to appeal to white buyers more so than African American buyers - The Supremes at the Copa for example. Just classing up the acts and going for a classier image — making them more palatable to whites — but not losing the blacks, but just knowing that that's where the money was, that's where the big bucks are. It's not only smart business, it's very smart business. And Berry did it successfully; he paved the way for Diana to eventually become a movie star...

*One final and more philosophical question. The music critic Theodor Adorno is credited with saying that the music-listening public does not actually know what it likes — it has to be told, given tastes externally. What do you think of this claim? Who dictates the public's taste in music?

I disagree. I have enough confidence in the public that it knows its own taste. Berry used to say, if it ain't in the grooves, it ain't got it. Adorno was right, but so was Berry. Adorno was basically defining it in terms of the great classicists — I don't know that he was applying it to popular styles.

*Can you recommend anyone else who could be a source on Motown and its P.R. efforts?

I worked pretty single-handedly. You could send a note to Mort Persky to see how it went on the journalism side of things. But in terms of PR, I did it all myself — it was my paranoia. I didn't trust anyone else to do the job I knew I could do. Remember the Baroque press releases?

Talent is your key word. These were some of the most talented people of the generation. Marvin Gaye was a genius. I'm still in awe of Berry--almost 50 years later and I'm still in awe.

**Al Abrams – Consent for Motown Memoirs Manuscript
Interview & Book Use
Interviewer: Dylan Morris, University of Michigan
Mark Clague, Ph.D., University of Michigan
Living Music project of the University of Michigan**

Al at the Bentley Library, University of Michigan

Al speaking to University of Michigan Music Students on Motown & Music & his global media escapades

Jobete Music Company, Inc.

2648 WEST GRAND BOULEVARD
DETROIT 8, MICHIGAN

TRinity 1-3340

July 19, 1960

FOR IMMEDIATE RELEASE

Att: Ira Howard
Editorial: Music Dept.
Cashbox Magazine
1721 Broadway Ave.
New York, New York

"TAMLA NAMES ABRAMS PR HEAD"

DETROIT—Cleffer Berry Gordy Jr. upped Al Abrams, former national promotion director for Gordy's Pubbery Jobete Music Co; To Director of advertising and public relations for his twin diskerys TAMLA and MOTOWN RECORDS. In addition to his new duties Abrams will continue to supervise all promotion for both labels. Abrams currently is seeking four experienced promo men to rep the diskery on the road. He can be reach daily at TR 13340.

Label is currently hot with "WAY OVER THERE" by the MIRACLES, who broke into the top 100 with "BAD GIRL" about this time last year; and is currently preparing new singles for immediate release by BARRETT (MONEY THAT'S WHAT I WANT) STRONG and thrush MABLE JOHN, sister of hot R & B artist LITTLE WILLIE JOHN who was recently inked by Gordy. Albums are also in preperation by the MIRACLES and BARRETT STRONG.

In addition to managing the above Gordy manages MARV JOHNSON, currently riding high with 2 sides in the HOT 100.

Al selling Motown with the guys!

Al, Brian/Eddie Holland & Michaela

Mary Wilson and Al.

Miss Martha Reeves, Suzi Quatro & Al

The Contours with Al and their Manager.

Cynthia Lennon, Al & Sherie Rae Parker

**Robert Bateman and Al, Cotton Candy Symposium
University of Michigam**

Mickey Stevenson & Al

To Al Love - Miracles

5

Script for a Record Label Television Series

**HYPE! Music Dramedy Detroit TV Pitch by Al Abrams
(2014-2015)**

HYPE! is a Dramedy. HYPE! is based upon the memories of my life. Acting as press agent for Motown, my responsibility was to sell a Black music owned label as crossover music to the world. Simply put - all I had to do was "SPIN" the VINYL!

Berry Gordy, Motown's founder, entrusted me with a PR job requiring nothing short of music miracles. I surmised it best in one phrase, "If it's a hit; it's a miracle!"

While America was on fire struggling with the Civil Rights Movement, the kids of Motown were jamming, eating hamburgers, drinking coca colas and creating a music revolution unbeknownst that they were also making history. The kids who grew up Motown together never acknowledged skin color or racial barriers. They loved music; breathed music; and made music.

They may have produced Gold records; but their friendships are the real Gold standard.

HYPE! encourages viewers to vicariously relive those moments and share those music dreams with Detroit's "M-Kids". The storylines are fresh, original, honest, hilarious, crazy, happy, sad and poignant. And they are being told by the one kid who had to put the HYPE! in the HIT! ... ME.

HYPE! is a musical memoir of scenarios where black and white kids came of age together. Their passion for music became their compassion for each other.

HYPE! The most relevant factor and the most overlooked in the creation of the Motown record label is in the mix of kids who helped build it into an international music genre. Music is HYPE! HYPE! is Music. And music motivates, inspires and changes lives.

The successful HBO hit series, Entourage, used Ari Gold as a passionate Hollywood agent to the stars; consider me as the passionate PR Go-To-Guy who helped create the HYPE! for Motown's stars. Let's "HYPE!" a television music hit.

HYPE!

Episode 1

It's 1959 in Detroit. A hip, happening city at that time that rivaled New York and Chicago. It was a city very much divided between black and white. However, I seemed to bridge that gap being a white Jewish boy, who happened to love black music. When you first meet me, I am hustling 16-year-old working two jobs. I stocked records at Handleman Co., a record distributor, and also worked in the mailroom at McCann Erickson, a large advertising agency. My perk for working in the mailroom was that I was able to use a slick 1958 Buick to drive around on weekends.

With my limited funds, I would head over to Joe Von Battle's record store in the Black Bottom neighborhood of Detroit to buy 78 vinyl RPM's of rhythm and blues music. When I got fired from Handleman Co. for lying about my age, I got the bright idea to become a record mogul and record my own song to sell to a record label. I enlisted my friend, Sonny, to help me. We wrote a song, rounded up some musicians (later known as the Funk Brothers), corralled some equipment and used the mother's upstairs flat as a recording studio. I even hired half-naked shake dancers from Toledo, Ohio (a wild town just over the Michigan border) to shake their booty and give the musicians inspiration and set a cool vibe for the session.

My mom, Mildred Abrams, came home from her work at a local deli, to complaining neighbors, and loud music emanating from her apartment. She opened the door to find me, Sonny, and a host of black musicians and dancers. She isn't pleased. But Al and Sonny have their recording. Now, they just have to sell it.

Episode 2

Sonny and I go party-hopping, excited about the prospect of becoming record moguls. I always saw a party as an opportunity to get two things: women and records. And we have the 1958 Buick from my advertising gig. We cruise the streets listening to DJ Larry Dixon on the black station WCHB. We find a party and join in. We couldn't score with any women. However, I spotted a stack of records. When the lights go down for a slow dance and make-out session, I raced over and grabbed the 45's and stuck them under my shirt. When I was spotted, I offered what little money I had for them. Left with the 45's in the Buick.

We woke up early the next morning to drive to Chicago to take the acetate of our recording session to try and lease it to Chess Records. We did stop off in Toledo to sneak into a strip club. Sonny was nervous, but I talked our way in. I wanted to order a couple of drinks, but Sonny chickens out and we left.

As we cruised on the Ohio Turnpike toward Chicago, we got pulled over for speeding. The Highway Patrol Officer tells them they will have to follow him to the station for going over 80 mph without a license. Al shows him the record and tells him that they have an important meeting in Chicago to sell their record. The officer spots Al's expensive watch, he suggests they can make a trade. They avoid the ticket and arrest, and head off to Chicago. They are late for their appointment, but Phil Chess gives their song a listen. He says he'll let them know.

Episode 3

I returned the Buick to the ad agency 6 am on Monday morning. When the Mad Men-like ad exec gets into the car, he hears Black Rhythm and Blues blaring from WCHB. "What the fuck kind of music is this?" he screams at me when he finds out I borrowed the car.

He gave me a lesson on what type of music is appropriate.

Sonny was supposed to follow-up with Phil Chess. I get on Sonny about following up as we head over after work to see WXYZ-TV DJ Mickey Shorr where he holds court at Darby's Deli. Shorr would always have a huge stack of 45 rpm records that he got from promotion men but couldn't play on the air because of his station's tight play list. So, he'd give them to kids like me. While hanging around trying to get free records, Shorr mentions to Sonny that he knows a guy with a small record label looking for someone to drive around his recording artists to record hops. Sonny says he might be interested, so Shorr gave him the address and the guy to see. His name is Berry Gordy.

I and Sonny are go to a record hop that evening. This one is at a Catholic High School. Billy K, another friend from the neighborhood joins us. It's where the teenagers dance while the record labels promote their artists by having them attend and lip synch while the DJ plays their songs. The DJ's get paid by the venue, the kids pay to get in and dance, and the labels get their records played and hopefully bought by the kids who hear the music. It's a win, win for everyone.

I and Sonny have a good time, dancing, meeting girls. It's where I meet Jane Fisher, the daughter of a well-known financier and I ask her out. She says she'll think about it.

Shorr is DJ'ing and reminds Sonny to go see Berry about the job. "You'll have fun," he tells him. Sonny says he'll go.

Episode 4

Sonny headed over to my flat and wakes me up. He shows me the address 1719 Gladstone in Detroit's inner city. He says he is too scared to go alone, but he wants a job. I agreed to go with him. We head over to the other side of town. We arrive at the small house and meet Berry Gordy and his girlfriend Raynoma.

Berry interviewed Sonny for the position, while I listened to some of their music on a record player. At the end of the interview, Berry is interested in hiring Sonny. However, Sonny isn't that keen on the position and working in this bad neighborhood with a bunch of black people he is not comfortable around. After Sonny more or less turns down the job, I, excited by the music I had been listening to, blurts out, "I'd be interested." Berry wasn't too interested, so to blow me off, he tosses me a record. It's a song called, "Teenage Sweetheart" recorded by a Yugoslavian dishwasher. "If you can get that played on the air, I'll give you the job," Berry snickers.

I took the record and his challenge seriously. After we leave, Berry and Raynoma fall into a fit of laughter. "We'll never see that white boy again," Berry howls. The next day was Memorial Day. I had an idea. I heard DJ Larry Dixon of WCHB was going to be broadcasting remotely for the Memorial Day holiday from a sponsor's location on Tireman Road. I am taking the record there and try to get Dixon to play it. I got my friend, Billy, to cme with me. We spent four hours out in the hot sun, badgering Dixon and trying to get him to play the record. My antics and humor finally get to Dixon.

Finally, as they are closing down the broadcast, Dixon takes pity on me and plays the record. At the same time, Berry and Raynoma are driving to a picnic on Belle Isle. As Berry tunes in the car radio, he hears "Teenage Sweetheart." Berry nearly drives his car into the Detroit River. He looked at Raynoma who is dumbfounded herself. "Holy shit! The white boy got the record played! He must be some kind of promotion genius!" Raynoma nods her head in agreement. "You know we're gonna' have to give him a job." Berry can't believe it.

Episode 5

I showed up at the Gordy's flat with a shit-eating grin. Berry and Raynoma welcomed me upstairs while they were still in bed. They offered me a job in promotions and publicity for $15 per week and all the chili I could eat. I gladly accepted. Berry and Raynoma told me to be at their house the next day.

Only one problem, I don't know anything about publicity. But I did know a lot about Tony Curtis. I go to the movie with Billy and Sonny to watch "Sweet Smell of Success" again. I took note of Curtis' portrayal of Sidney Falco, the sleazy PR agent. He has a role model.

I showed up at the flat and met Marv Johnson, Eddie Holland, Robert Bateman, and Smokey Robinson. I was asked to outfit them for a TV-show appearance. So, I go to Hot Sam's Fashions and work out a deal to get them tuxedos. I also work out a deal to get one for myself and Mike Powers, the Yugoslavian dishwasher turned teen idol.

I try my PR skills to try to get Powers a write-up. I pull my Tony Curtis act at the Windsor Star. When the Star goes for it, I corral

Powers into wearing a fancy silk tuxedo from Hot Sam's Fashions, which is more befitting a 1970's pimp than a 1950's teen idol for a photo shoot. The shoot goes well, and I take that as a sign to wear one of the pimp suits for my date with Jane Fisher, who has finally agreed to go out with me. When, I showed up at the Fisher mansion, Mr. Fisher opened the door. "What the hell are you doing here?" he asked incredulous. "Going out with your daughter," I replied. "The hell you're not," says Fisher as he slams the door on me. Perhaps, I do belong more in the inner city than with the country club set.

Episode 6

I climbed into Berry's car on Sunday evening. We cruise the streets of Detroit aimlessly listening to WJLB, which carried the live broadcasts of various inner city churches. I dubbed it "Gospel Cruis'in". We happened upon an interesting singing voice. We figure out which church the broadcast was emanating from and head over. A particular girl catches our attention and we head to Ebenezer AME Church. The three head into the church and listen to the choir. We picked out the voice that intrigued us and we meet a young girl. Berry handed her a business card and invited her to audition for Smokey and Robert Bateman.

I meet up with Eddie Holland, who I have to take to a record hop. I showed up in my convertible as it starts to rain. I can't get the top up on the convertible. I delivered a soaking wet Eddie to his record hop. Eddie is somewhat of a teen idol and the girls go crazy over him. Larry Dixon and Bob Greene are DJ'ing, and after the hop, Dixon asked us if we want to grab a smoke after the show. Everybody smoked in that era, so it was only a natural thing to do.

A mob of crazy girls jumped Eddie after the show and started ripping off his clothes. I had to get him out of there. We get in Dixon's T-Bird. We drop off Eddie and drive out to Willow Run Airport. I'm thinking why the hell do you need to drive out to the middle of nowhere to smoke. Dixon pulls out a reefer (as it was called back then) and introduces it. They head back to the city, high as kites.

Episode 7

I began working on writing bios for the Artists at Motown as no one had thought to do it before. I worked on getting background information on Marv Johnson. As we get to know each other, I taught Marv some Yiddish words. Meanwhile, Berry works on getting Marv's song, licensed by United Artists.

Marv has an appearance on CKLW in Windsor, Canada, across the border from Detroit. I, Berry, Marv, Robert and John Oden, Berry's driver, go to the show. Marv sings on the show and causes a sensation. We drink and party in Windsor after the show. On the way back, we got stopped by a Customs officer. He questions us, when he asks who they have in the car, Berry replies, "Nobody here but us niggers." The officer shines a light in my face. "Okay," he said and lets us go. We start working on a new song for Marv and I contribute to the lyrics. By the time we arrive home we have written "I Love the Way You Love."

I meet Ann Merner and take her on a date. Berry tells me about how much girls like them to "eat their pussies." Al has never heard of such a thing remarking, "What is that some kind of African cannibal ritual?" Berry tells him to try it on his date with Ann, but Al just kisses her goodnight. Marv records the song we wrote and I have my first songwriting credit at Motown. It's Berry's way of giving something back to me since he can't pay me much in the way of salary.

Episode 8

Berry reads in Jet Magazine a story about the plight of pioneer black actor and comedian Stepin Fetchit. He was living in poverty in Chicago. Berry sends me to go and find him and ask him about recording a comedy album. I head off to Chicago to track down Fetchit. I took Sonny along so we can stop at Chess Records to see about our song with Phil Chess, as Sonny never followed up like he was supposed to do.

Once in Chicago, I play PI and track down Fetchit's real name through a lead at the post office. I found Fetchit living in squalor despite the fact he was the first black Hollywood star and millionaire in the 1930's. Sonny gets word that Phil Chess liked our harmonies but won't release the record. He said he was done with the record business.

Meanwhile, Berry and Janie Bradford, a secretary at Motown, work out the lyrics for the song "Money" for Barrett Strong to record. I brought Fetchit back to Detroit where they try and record a comedy album with him. However, Fetchit is more interested in discussing his conversion to Islam than making people laugh. Berry gives Fetchit some money to help him out, but decided not to release the record.

Episode 9

Berry and Barrett Strong play the song "Money" for me. They all agree it is a smash. They decide to promote Barrett and the song heavily. I drive Barrett to Gary, Indiana for a show. During the show, I met a gorgeous groupie. The show is a success. When Barrett comes off stage, he spots the two of them together and heads over. Barrett starts hitting on the girl. Barrett and Al get into a confrontation, which ends by Barrett grabbing the girl as he snarls "I'm the star, you work for me," and slugged me. Pissed, I took the bus home to Detroit and left Barrett to drive himself home. Berry was angry when he heard about Barrett's behavior, but he still believed in Barrett's career and they have to get "Money" on the air.

Berry asks me who is the best DJ to break the record and I told him that for this one we have to go straight to the top: Alan Freed at WABC in New York. Berry asks me to figure out how Freed will play the record.

I had never been to New York, but I knew some of the other promotion men in Detroit might give me answers. The "Promo Men" as they were called, worked distribution for the major record labels. They hung out at a coffee shop across from WJBK on Second

Avenue. I had seen them before, but never talked to them or been invited to join them. I headed over and asked if any of them knew how to get Alan Freed to play a record. They looked at me and laughed.

Eventually, Dave Fox called me over and told me that you need to slip Freed a $100 bill when you give him the record and that's not for playing it on the air. It was just for his expert opinion about the merits of the record.

I informed Berry. Hee decides we have to go to New York. Berry would meet with United Artists about expanding his deal for distribution and I would go meet Alan Freed.

Barrett returns to Hitsville. Berry chews him out for fighting with Al over the groupie. Barrett apologizes, and then confides, "Damn bitch gave me the clap!"

Al and Berry laugh hysterically.

Episode 10

I took my first plane ride and first trip to NYC with Berry and Raynoma. Berry and Raynoma usually stay in Harlem but Berry thinks it's important to project a successful image. If anyone at United Artists needs to reach them while in town, he doesn't want them leaving messages at a hotel in Harlem.

So, we stop at the Park Sheraton in Midtown. However, they only have enough money for one hotel room. Berry says they will be staying. Berry and Raynoma go to meet the executives at United Artists. They had success with Marv Johnson and Berry wants them to expand distribution to Motown's other artists.

Meanwhile, I head over to WABC with a $100 bill and Barrett Strong's "Money" on an oversize acetate dub. When I got to the station, I'm ushered into a long waiting room. There is a long bench with a row of other promotion men packed with records in hand.

I waited a long time and finally I get my turn with Freed.

I'm ushered into the studio. While another record is playing on air, Freed spins "Money" on another turntable. He listens to the first couple of verses and then turns it off and stares at me while I'm handing him the $100 bill. "I'm the first in the country to have this, right?" asks Freed. I assured him that they came to him first. "I'm gonna' wail on this right, away," he announced to me. As I am ushered out of the studio, I can hear Alan Freed talking on the air, "Just give me money, that's what I want." And Barrett's song is blasting out of the speakers. I rushed back to the Park Sheraton. When I arrived, Berry tells me that their meeting was also a success.

Tired, Berry told me to take the bed, while he and Raynoma sleep on the floor. I didn't feel comfortable with this and I said we'd flip a coin for it. I won the coin toss, but I told Berry that I lost.. Berry and Raynoma slept in the bed. I slept on the floor. I was awoken in the morning by a black maid who is shocked to see a white boy sleeping on the floor while the black guests are in the bed. I went back to sleep. When I woke up again, a gaggle of hotel maids all came to peek in their room and view the strange sight.

Future Seasons of HYPE! Season 2

The Motortown Revue in D.C. becomes a success. I meet a young black singer on the bill and convinced her to come to Detroit to audition for Berry.

Robert Bateman helps write "Please Mr. Postman" which becomes a huge hit for the Marvelettes. I became the road manager for The Satintones and The Miracles. I experienced my first large scale PR success when I turned a near riot at a Miracles show in St. Louis into national publicity.

I continued my promotion efforts by hooking up DJ's with dinner dates and favors.

Robert Bateman discovered the young girls known as The Primettes at a talent show in Windsor, Ontario. Berry doesn't want to sign the girls at first. Instead, one of them becomes a secretary at Motown. Marvin Gaye joined Motown as a session drummer, and performing at the 20 Grand,

I met a girl known as "The Redhead," a 6- foot gorgeous, sex-crazed groupie, who becomes a Motown regular. To get Milt Grant of Washington Bandstand to let Motown artists appear in his segregated TV dance party show in 1960, I took her to D.C. to close the deal. She pretending to be my wife at dinner, Grant spent the whole night eyeing her cleavage and then agreed to every artist I suggested. I was grateful she helped. She was kind.

A 17- year-old Mary Wells approached Berry at Detroit's Twenty Grand club with a song that she had intended for Jackie Wilson to maybe record. However, a tired Berry insisted Wells sing the song in front of him. Thereafter, Berry convinced Wells to join Motown as a singer/songwriter.

After hanging out at Hitsville one night, Berry suggested I take the uptight Sonny down to John R Road and "get him some pussy." Sonny came back crying, he told Berry that the hooker stole his expensive ring. Berry told him to come back the next day and he'll have the ring. Ever connected to the streets, the next day when Sonny arrived, Berry had his ring.

I took Billy K backstage to a Dick Clark show at the Fox Theatre featuring Chubby Checker, Dion and the Belmonts, and Fabian.

Season 3

The Primettes were re-named The Supremes and Berry tries to get them a hit record. However, their first recordings were a disaster.

I wined and dined visiting DJ's at the 20 Grand, along with record promotion man Al Valente. We visited DJ Bob Parkinson in Toledo and convinced his listeners to support the record label and our artists.

The Miracles brought Motown its first ever gold record for selling a million copies with the song "Shop Around."

Berry puts Eddie Holland together with his brother Brian and Lamont Dozier to work writing songs/producing for other Motown artists. Brian had previously been working with Robert Bateman.

A group of singers later known as The Contours begin working in the mailroom at Motown.

I got The Miracles and Marv Johnson a big newspaper story in the Detroit Times, the first time Motown had gotten substantial coverage in a "white" periodical.

Plying DJ's with round-trip air tickets to NY (which were dirt cheap for weekends) or giving them a box of 100 records direct from the factory helped. One DJ took the records to a big Detroit mob-run juke box operator to sell them. A distributor got pissed-off that such actions were skewing record sales and pitting them against mobsters.

Berry releases, "Don't Let Him Shop Around" as an answer to The Miracles' hit.

I went to Chicago to promote it on Jim Lounsbury's TV show. When Jim told me that his wife was performing at a country western club in Kankakee, I then felt obligated to go. Packed in a Cadillac with a bunch of others for the ride, I ended up with a gorgeous PR girl sitting on my lap and had a hard time containing my hard-on. During a quick stop for gas, the girl returned with no panties on.

Season 4

Jimmy Ruffin (later of The Temptations) joined Motown as a session singer.

Berry signed the Supremes to Motown Records as they finally started showing signs of real talent. Raynoma helped Berry negotiate the purchase of 2644-2646 West Grand Boulevard to house Jobete

Publishing, along with the sales, shipping and public relations of Motown.

Martha Reeves was hired as a secretary at Motown.
The Temptations record "Oh Mother of Mine."

Berry found that Martha Reeves had real talent and puts her together with The Marvelettes.

Tony Orlando, then a record executive, comes to town on a promo tour, I set him up with a girl and they go a double dinner date.

After seeing "Psycho" with Bob Patton, a younger promo man that I befriended, Patton decided to play a joke on me as we made our DJ rounds in the Midwest. Patton enlisted The Redhead to take the trip with us to help with the gag. While I and The Redhead take a rwalk to the end of a pier on a scenic spot on Lake Erie, Patton dresses up in a blonde wig and hurtles toward us with a rubber knife. I am so freaked I fell into Lake Erie. Patton and The Redhead had a hearty laugh at my expense.

I started to make more connections in the publishing and newspaper world, as my time was being spent more on publicity. In making a connection with Mort Persky, the

Sunday editor of The Detroit Free Press, the number two newspaper in Detroit, I and Berry take Mort and his wife on a tour of the streets of Detroit. We ended up in Detroit's Cass Corridor (known for its streetwalkers).

I worked on helping transition Motown's publicity from strictly black publications to the national major dailies with articles in Time, Life, Look, and the Saturday Evening Post.

When Al Aronowitz of the Saturday Evening Post came to Hitsville, for an interview I arranged, his first question to the Supremes is: "Which one of you is fucking Berry Gordy?" Berry is furious. Despite all the in roads in the white media, I still couldn't crack The Detroit News.

Season 5

After a string of hits, I finally got The Supremes on the cover of a TV Guide. This was the first time a black group ever appeared on this genre of national publications.

Berry formed The Vandellas with Martha Reeves to back up Marvin Gaye.

The Temptations make the move to Motown records and record, "Isn't She Pretty."

I meets some groupies at a record hop in Toledo where I was handing out promotional records with stickers that said, "Thanks for the Spin." It was perfect for DJ's and groupies alike.

As the company gets larger, Berry hires more staffers, including a stunning white girl from Australia. Ron Miller, composer of For Once in My Life for Stevie Wonder enlisted my help to get her fired for giving him the clap.

Berry hires Maxine Powell, who had been operating a finishing and modeling school, to prep the performers and transform Motown artists into polished professionals.

Berry signs The Four Tops, who recorded jazz standards and back up for the Supremes. Later, Berry enlists the Holland Brothers and Lamont Dozier to write songs for them.

Berry Gordy chose Diana Ross as the official lead singer of The Supremes, and they recorded the single "Where Did Our Love Go" a song by Holland-Dozier-Holland and originally intended for Martha Reeves.

Though they disliked the song, it reached Number One on Billboard while The Supremes toured as part of Dick Clark's Caravan of Stars.

HYPE! CHARACTERS – Names to be changed for TV Show.

AL ABRAMS - Brash, fast-talking, wise-cracking, quick on his feet. The key player in story. Eighteen at start of story (1959), but passing for older. Tall, thin, paid great attention to hair. Looked a lot like younger David Schwimmer of Friends or even a much younger Jeff Goldblum. His screen idol was Tony Curtis's character, Sidney Falco, in Sweet Smell of Success. Abrams turned to that characterization when he had to start getting press coverage for the Motown artists. More than a half-century later, Motown historians still describe his style as "maddeningly innovative." Although white and Jewish, he was quickly adopted into the all-black milieu of both the Gordy and Motown families where he rapidly absorbed the culture. A connoisseur of fine women, he was often found in the company of one or more stunning model-like females. Also, kind-hearted to those who needed help.

BERRY GORDY, JR. - A wiry, quick-witted, confident, former Golden Gloves boxer with a warm, attractive personality that others responded to favorably. He is free-spirited, restless, and tends to fly from one thing to the next. He loves women, and is definitely a player. He founded the Rayber Music Writing Company (a combination of the names of Berry and his then-fiancé Raynoma) which, for a fee, would help anyone write, produce, and record a record. They advertised on a local radio and produced a slew of unforgettable tracks. Eventually, Berry wanted to make and produce his own records, and so he and Raynoma would drive around Detroit looking for talent. They would scope out the churches and clubs, and soon they started to put together a group that would become the backbone of Motown. Their first label, Tamla, was located at 1719 Gladstone in Detroit. In early 1959, Berry Gordy borrowed from $800 from his family for the recording, pressing and, promotional cost of the planned release of "Come to Me" by Marv Johnson. It was recorded at the famous United Sound Studios on Second, and the record was soon picked up by United Artists. They were on their way. The Jobete Music Publishing Company was also launched that same year, and in the spring of 1959, Al Abrams joined the crew. Berry pretty much became Al's surrogate older brother.

They would spend all day and night together working, and learning about each other's cultures. Since Gordy lived and worked in the same buildings, work and friendship became enmeshed. They would spend a couple hours each night sitting in Gordy's living quarters on the second floor of Hitsville, talking, joking, and sharing everything. Women were always a topic of discussion. "You know, they really like it when you eat their pussies," Berry said one time. Abrams had no idea what he was talking about. Turning to Gordy, bewildered, Abrams looked at him and said, "Is that some kind of cannibal ritual from Africa?" Gordy laughed his head off. "Just try it."

WILLIAM "BILL" "SMOKEY" ROBINSON - A musical genius that was then still a work in-progress, he was a skinny light-skinned African-American kid that was just exploding with talent. Possessor of that unmistakable voice and constantly writing down lyrics for the many songs spinning through his head, he was a warm and welcoming factor. We shared the same birthday although he was and amazingly still is a year older than me. I quickly found the key to his intense sense of humor and after a short time realized I had the ability to reduce him to hysterical fits of laughter simply by reciting the real names of people such as that of Hosea Hornbuckle, a former Central High classmate. While I was driving the Miracles to a show in St. Louis, I noticed that once we passed Terre Haute, the names on the rural mailboxes became even more Germanic and unusual and if I read them off they would actually put Smokey on the floor of the cramped VW bus. I eventually was able to mimic Smokey's response of an elongated and repeated "Oh, man" enough to make him laugh. He was always considerate and caring as were the other members of the Miracles, especially Claudette, his future wife. Still, he was a major chick magnet and we occasionally prowled the 20 Grand. I was happy that he was included in that first pivotal Detroit Times newspaper story in 1960.

BARRETT STRONG - Edgy, cocky, competitive and highly volatile, he still had a lot of the rough edges of the street. He knew he was on to something big with "Money" and that I was doing everything I could to make it happen. We competed for the attention of the same groupies on the road, culminating in the infamous incident where Barrett got the girl and I got slugged by him, but he got the bonus of getting a dose of clap from her. If it wasn't an issue of competing for a woman's attention, we were fine. But when it came down to the game of who would take home the prize, Barrett tended to play for keeps. Yet, we both won more than our fair share. Emotionally, he was the polar opposite of Smokey. He was the first Motown artist to be interviewed by a mainstream white DJ when I took him to a remote broadcast hosted by Chuck Daugherty (see below) on WXYZ radio.

ROBERT BATEMAN - One of the most underrated talents of the early days, he was actually the company's first recording engineer. His disability, a shriveled right hand, never kept him from being as cocky as the rest of us with a willingness to take on the world and win. Possessor of a distinctive bass voice, he was a member of the Rayber Voices and later the Satintones. As a songwriter, Berry, who had an incredible innate ability to encourage songwriter/producers, teamed him with Brian Holland as Brianbert, and they were responsible for the company's iconic first megahit, "Please Mr. Postman" by the Marvelettes. As a company talent scout, Robert discovered the group much as he had discovered the four girls who sang as the Primettes, and later became the Supremes. It was Robert who had to deal with my initial refusal to ride in – much less drive – the company's VW bus. He always wanted to sleep with Berry's wife Raynoma so he never passed an opportunity to subtly let her know who Berry was screwing at any particular time of the day. Robert and I would both become frustrated over what we perceived as a lack of growth by the company and would walk out. Once I actually threw all my addressograph stencils up in the air not thinking the metal plates would now fall back onto my head. I couldn't come back and face anyone for a month. But I'd come back. One day, Robert decided not to – and didn't.

THE HOLLAND BROTHERS, EDDIE AND BRIAN - Both of them welcomed me to the company and made me feel like family from Day One. As Brian told me at Esther Gordy Edwards's funeral in 2011, they never even considered me to be white. I drove Eddie to record hops and he put up with being delivered to one hop sopping wet when my convertible top balked at going up during a sudden downpour. Brian was always the more outgoing, with a great sense of humor. Eddie was more pensive and serious. They were part of my famous moving team for DJ Chuck Daugherty and never balked at any promo idea I'd come up with. And they were always there later for media interviews – real troupers. Eddie sounded so much like Jackie Wilson that Berry used him to record all of the demos of the songs he'd penned for Jackie. We're all about a year or two apart in age.

MARV JOHNSON - He was already pretty savvy when I met him, maybe because he was a couple of years older than the rest of us kids. He hung out a lot with Billy too. We were impressed with his knowledge of Yiddish – which he broached to me one day by saying, "I know I'm a schvartza." That endeared him to me. He never acted like the star he was already on the way to becoming. He was just a fun, down-to-earth kind of guy who deserved so much better than the hand Berry eventually dealt him. That's the making of another true Motown tragedy. Berry opted not to renew Marv's contract in 1969 but the company never told Marv and so he continued to come in to the studio daily and write and record. When the 1972 move to LA came, he was not asked to move with the company and that's when he learned the truth about his contract. Berry could really be a motherfucker when it came to rewarding loyalty. We need to portray him warts and all. The one thing you can't lose sight of is that he was once a pimp and when things were tough he once even pimped out his wife Raynoma. That's important drama.

LARRY DIXON - The mellow bass-voiced African-American Detroit DJ who played such a pivotal role in the Motown story. At best, a sleazy motherfucker. At worst, a sleazy motherfucker. There was never an in-between, but you took him as he was. Probably six to ten years older than me. Thin, dark and not particularly attractive. He had made the first contact for Berry with United Artists for the Marv Johnson record and never forgot an opportunity to remind Berry about it. He is also the DJ who played the Mike Powers record that got me hired. And he never let me forget it either. It was Larry who taught me how to smoke joints while we drove up and down I-94 from Motown to the old Willow Run Airport in his black T-Bird to evade cops. Interestingly, he did the same thing for my DJ friend Bob Greene (see below) once I introduced them. Larry was probably as close to me as he allowed himself to get with any white promo man because we shared a music avocation. In later years, I'd give Larry an airline ticket to New York or a box of 100 records he could peddle to the juke box operators just for old-time's sake.

CHUCK DAUGHERTY - The affable Irish-American DJ whom I could talk into doing anything for a laugh. Two sides to this guy who was one of my most loyal friends. He broke the rules by interviewing Barrett Strong and playing "Money" on WXYZ. In return, Holland-Dozier-Holland and I were his moving crew when he moved from Grosse Pointe to the wilds of Farmington Hills. That's where he stashed the wife and kids we eventually had to rescue from starvation when he abandoned them to take off to LA with a 16-year-old blonde groupie. I talked him into doing his hair green for a St. Patrick's Day promotion and he couldn't get the green out for months afterward. That was Chuck that Bob Greene and I, disguised as doctors, wildly wheeled up and down the corridors of a hospital. We genuinely liked him despite his faults. I'd often – too often – hang out in the studio with him while he broadcast his all-night radio show and not just because he'd sneak in a few of my records. He'd do that even if I wasn't there. But I could borrow his big black Lincoln Continental and cruise the clubs for a couple of hours trolling for chicks, although what I'd find was never quite worth the extra effort. I didn't need the big car to score. Daugherty was about ten years older than me.

BOB GREENE - Probably my closest white DJ friend. He respected my mother, (as did Berry) and Berry liked him. Bob was a main part of our group that would go to the 20 Grand or the Minor Key to see and hear the legendary artists perform. We kind of thought of Bob as being asexual although in retrospect he was probably the first homosexual I knew. But that issue was never raised. Bob was not just a fan of the music, he had a great knowledge and respect for all things Jewish which made him a mensch in my eyes. Maybe six years older than me, thin, slight, blond hair, glasses. In retrospect, he looked awfully German!

SANFORD "SONNY" FREED - He was my other very close friend. It was Sonny who was my partner in my recording session with the Funk Brothers in my mother's (see below) living room – complete with a Toledo shake dancer. Sonny and I then drove to Chicago to lease the record to Chess Records. That's the trip on which my expensive wristwatch wound up on the hand of an Ohio State Trooper. It was Sonny who went with me to see Mickey Shorr at the deli when we first heard about Berry Gordy. Sonny didn't want to go alone into the inner city alone so I skipped work and went with him to 1719 Gladstone that week. Berry wanted to hire Sonny, Sonny didn't want the job, I did, and Berry gave me the Mike Powers disc to get rid of me telling Raynoma (see below) that "we'll never see that white boy again." At first, Sonny didn't care much that I had been hired, but as Motown became more glamorous, Sonny began to get jealous, eventually turning on me and accusing me of stealing the job from him because he was entitled to it as Berry's first choice. Eventually, it helped contribute to his tragically committing suicide on the I-75 freeway.

WILLIAM "BILLY" KINGSTON - Hipper than Sonny, but on more solid ground than Abrams. Second best buddy, but later took top spot. Thin, good looking. Couple of years older than Abrams. Abrams's closest friend since they were in grade school. I introduced him early on to the sounds of Black music, playing my precious 78's that I'd buy on Hastings Street. When I got hired by Berry I quickly introduced Billy to him and the members of my new family. Berry liked hanging out with Billy. We hung out together with Marv Johnson and I got Billy backstage at a Dick Clark Show at the Fox Theatre featuring the (white) Philly Sound guys: Frankie Avalon, Fabian, Dion and the Belmonts and Chubby Checker even before I started at Motown. Because Billy hung out with me at the Hitsville Studios, on super slow summer days, Berry told me to take the afternoon off and I'd go out to Kensington Lake with Billy. And Billy got to know all of the various women I was dating.

RAYNOMA LILES GORDY - The ACTUAL First Lady of Motown! Petite, brainy, great and quick conversationalist. Dyed blonde hair. Light skinned. Very attractive and sexy. Think Beyonce. Perfect match for Berry. Instantly made me feel welcome at Motown letting me into the private lives of her and Berry. Granted me access to Berry even if it meant my showing up in their bedroom to wake him up. A member of the Rayber Voices with a great ear for talent, the role Raynoma played in Motown's success has always been downplayed by Berry and his supporters. It would not have happened without her. She scouted the Hitsville studio location and made the deal to buy our first recording equipment. She was at 1719 Gladstone when I came there with Sonny and in the car on Belle Isle with Berry when the Mike Powers record was played on the air.

MILDRED ABRAMS - Think Hollywood casting for a Jewish mother. The actress who played Rhoda Morgenstern's mother on the Mary Tyler Moore show even looked and talked like her. Tolerated and supported her son in his craving for Black Music. Didn't panic when she came home to find the full Funk Brothers and a shake dancer playing in her living room. Although the remainder of my family wrote me off as lost to the schvartzes she never lost her faith in me and what I was doing. Berry asked me to teach him a few words in Yiddish so he could talk with her on the phone when he would call the house looking for me. Bob Greene was very respectful to her. I probably couldn't have been as cocky and self-assured were it not for her support. She met many of the women I was dating and was never judgmental. Early in life both my parents taught me to be color blind. I may have carried it a little further than my mother had hoped, but she never admonished me. And yes, I'd come home every night when I was in town. But talking women out of spending the night in my bed before my mother came home from work was often a challenge. When she moved to California to take care of her sister, I would mail her copies of all the Motown stories that mentioned me. After she died, I found them in her apartment, she had saved every single one of them. Following major characters are introduced later (1964-66 newspaper /magazine publicity era)

MORT PERSKY - The Detroit Free Press Sunday editor who adopted Motown and made us "Our Supremes." Father of actress Lisa Jane Persky ("When Harry Met Sally") and future husband of Judith Rossner ("Waiting for Mr. Goodbar"). When I brought Mort and his then-wife Yolanda to meet Berry, the topic somehow got on the subject of hookers on Detroit's Cass Corridor. Yolanda was disbelieving, but wanted to see for herself. So, Mort and I put her on the floor in the back seat of my car and covered her with a blanket as we flagged down hookers and discussed prices. One of the hookers looked at the back seat and said, "Yeah, but my price will be higher if I have to do your freak under the blanket." Years later, Persky, while editing Playboy, meets Berry Gordy at Hugh Hefner's house post-1972 when Berry says "Detroit, Where's that?"

BARBARA HOLLIDAY - Detroit Free Press columnist played major role

MARK STERN - One of the young Jewish guys who published the temporary Detroit strike paper and published the world's first news story on the Supremes breaking out with a Number One Hit.

ARNOLD S. HIRSCH - Jewish Detroit News writer (the guy who taught Barbra Streisand to drive) who was on the competition track with Persky to see which paper does the first post-strike story on the Supremes. That leads right into the famous TV magazine cover story.

ROY STEPHENS - African-American writer for the Michigan Chronicle who died right as we were making it big. Interesting for our transition from black weeklies to major dailies and Time, Life, Look, Saturday Evening Post

AL ARONOWITZ - Saturday Evening Post writer who asked Supremes "Which one of you is fucking Berry Gordy?" and who gave me Bob Dylan fake quote about Smokey Robinson.

M E M O R A N D U M

To: Al Abrams
From: Office of the President
Date: October 27, 1965
Re: Promotion - Smokey Robinson

Now that Smokey Robinson is one of the greatest songwriters of our time, I would like to start a promotion campaign for him. When writers such as Bob Dylan have a few hits, they are tremendously publicized.

Smokey has had many great records, such as "Shop Around," "My Guy," "Ain't That Peculiar," "I'll Be Doggoned," "My Girl" etc. There are even more important songs than those I've mentioned.

I would like for you to work out some kind of plan for his promotion and discuss your ideas with me.

Berry Gordy, Jr./gb

gb

6

Why Motown Black & White?

Why did I settle on Motown Black & White as the title for my music exhibit and private archive collection?

Music is a motivator. Music moves the world. It creates Movements that have and will forever challenge and change our world.

Music is also the surround sound for our personal lives. We breathe music. We create play lists to coincide with personal life events.

Motown: The Sound of Young America is the iconic slogan I created as Motown's young Detroit press officer. It's also a slogan used as a book title. This particular book never identifies the Motown slogan's author and its backroom story. It is an interesting sidebar ... sidestepped.

I felt that Motown's crossover sound needed to reach a target audience – teenagers. I conjured up the slogan so that Berry Gordy's Motown music would provide a sense of solidarity for American teenagers to integrate their dance floors. Gordy recognized the slogan's universal appeal and told me how much I meant to the success of Motown by integrating, not segregating people through music.

There is no simple solution to the integration of people in a world where segregation will always exist. Diversity is a complicated and never-ending vicious circle where humanity is challenged. It is a life-cycle that stays in a state of play.

Nothing of actual consequence is ever black or white. But, humanity is linked.

What is the color of dust? It is the color of one. It is the color of humanity. Dust is the inescapable global human equalizer.

Humanity matriculates from birth; to duration; to a final stage. Death is a stage walked into alone.

After death, some of us will be remembered by one or none; some of us remembered by a multitude; others of us will be remembered by the world.

However, when the dust settles, we become part of one world.

There are those amongst us who will be celebrated with elaborate funerals, pomp and circumstance and media covered obituaries. A gold-laden casket or urn will engulf us. There are those amidst us who will have an ordinary funeral with a few family and friends gathered to remember us. Our lifeless bodies will be placed into sacred cemetery ground or a Mausoleum vault.

But, many of us will be buried anonymously. We live within a global world where life altering circumstances changes our tombs. War, famine, disease, genocide, murder and catastrophic events claim us. Our human dust will settle into piles of rubble; makeshift landfills; ocean floors; killing fields or incinerators. We will forever share unmarked graves.

What is the color of global human dust? It is not black or white.

The MUSIC of our heart and soul will play on forever. MUSIC is, truly, neither Black nor White.

MUSIC unites and celebrates our universal HUMANITY and plays the colors of G-D'S SONG. G-D'S SONG is you, I and the diverse colors that surround our universe.

MUSIC PLAYS the COLOR OF DUST.

Thus, Motown Black & White is appropriate for my historical music collection and exhibit. The MB&W Collection/Exhibit would be a beautiful acquisition for a museum that celebrates music or incorporates music into its hallowed halls. Please inquire.

Motown Black & White Collection & Exhibit

Detroit Historical Museum, Detroit, MI USA

Stax-Volt Museum, Memphis, TN USA

SOULSVILLE FOUNDATION

April 21, 2017

Dear Motown Black & White Board of Trustees:

In 2016, the Stax Museum of American Soul Music hosted the *Motown Black & White* exhibition based on the life and career of legendary Motown Records PR man, Al Abrams. We began working with Mr. Abrams in 2015, shortly before his untimely passing. Like so many of the record company executives from the past, he had a deep appreciation for the music and the people who made it, and truly understood how meaningful it was to the wider population. While he often contended that "they were just kids making music," he also knew that Motown was part of something bigger going on in the United States during the 1960s. After parting ways with Motown, he began consulting with Motown's Southern "cousin," Stax Records in Memphis, Tennessee, working closely with their head of publicity, Deanie Parker. The two worked closely for nearly a year, with Abrams sharing his craft and business know-how with Ms. Parker and her team. Before long, Stax became a force in its own right in the music business. Al's lasting passion for Stax became clear when he arranged for us to receive a grant from the *Motown Black & White* program which greatly reduced our financial burden and allowed us to host the exhibition.

Al Abrams' role in the 1960s R&B world cannot be understated, so it was with great pleasure that we were able to present his story to our audience here at the Stax Museum. While prior stops on the exhibition's tour were able to offer a much larger space, Al's wife, Nancy, worked closely with us to curate an experience that would tell the whole story, fit into the space we had, and provide a strong visitor experience. The large-scale photographs transfixed visitors, while the sequin-and-feather-laden gowns worn by Mary Wilson and Martha Reeves transported them to another era of popular music. The exhibition provided a counterpoint to the Stax story we tell every day, too – two companies, driven by the same mission, but with two distinct sounds, two distinct ways of making records, and two different business models. While the exhibition left us in November 2016, we were disappointed to see it go.

The Stax Museum of American Soul Music wholeheartedly endorses the Motown Black & White exhibition, and recommends it for display in museum, historical societies, libraries, or community centers. The exhibition is informative, educational, and suitable for all ages, and will enhance an organization's exhibition and educational offerings.

Sincerely,

Jeff Kollath
Executive Director
Stax Museum of American Soul Music
jeff.kollath@soulsvillefoundation.org

**Lonnie & Al at the Ali Center MB&W Exhibit Opening
Ali Center, Lexingtom, KY USA**

Office of the President and Chief Executive Officer
DONALD E. LASSERE

June 19, 2014

To Whom It May Concern,

The Motown in Black and White exhibition held at the Ali Center in the fall of 2013 was composed of historical items from the personal collection of Al Abrams, the founding publicist of Motown and its public relations director during the label's glory days. From photos collected over the years to apparel worn by famous Motown artists, Abrams' archive of historical Motown items was unique and impressive.

Abrams, who worked with the likes of The Supremes, Marvin Gaye, Stevie Wonder, The Temptations, The Four Tops, Smokey Robinson and the Miracles, and many more, put together for Motown in Black and White an exhibit that focused on Motown, its music, its history and the diversity of its "family". The photographs, as the main feature, told a wonderful and uplifting story about kids who grew up Motown. They made music their passion; they made Civil Rights history together without even realizing it. And that is how Motown achieved its crossover sound, sold vinyl, and became a successful record label. These kids that grew up together had differences, but none that really mattered. Motown was not obsessed with skin color; but rather with making one sound for one world.

It was important for the Ali Center to display Motown in Black and White as a reminder of the cultural impact that Motown music had at its start and the influence that it maintains to this day. The Ali Center is guided by Muhammad Ali's Six Core Principles, one of which is Respect. Respect is a common theme throughout Motown in Black and White as Motown created a bridge to allow for learning and understanding of other people through the universal language of music. In addition to the powerful message communicated by the exhibit, Muhammad Ali is a huge fan of Motown himself; so there was great symmetry for us to host Motown in Black and White in the Center that bears his name.

Sincerely,

Donald E. Lassere
Donald E. Lassere
President and CEO

This exhibit is dedicated to Al Abrams, the man who collected the artifacts and assembled them into the display that you are about to enter.

He was the first employee hired by Berry Gordy, the founder of Motown Records. Al brought Motown Black & White to the Castle Museum because he thought Saginaw was ideal for the genre.

Sadly, he passed away on October 3, 2015, just three days before it opened to the public. Through this exhibit, his legacy lives on.

Castle Museum, Saginaw, MI USA

CASTLE MUSEUM
OF SAGINAW COUNTY HISTORY

Historical Society of Saginaw County
500 Federal Ave. • Saginaw, Michigan 48607
Telephone: (989) 752-2861 • Fax: (989) 752-1533

February 15, 2016

It is with great pleasure that we here at the Castle Museum of Saginaw County History heartily endorse the exhibit *Motown Black and White*. We hosted this engaging display for the last quarter of 2015 and we were very pleased with the outcome. The Premiere Party for *Motown Black and White* was the largest opening night crowd we had ever seen and the exhibit itself helped us break our all-time record for total visitors in 2015.

In addition, exhibit curators Al and Nancy Abrams were very personable and flexible with their time and knowledge. It is clear to us that they had the "inside track" on the history of Motown Records and how that iconic organization was formed and evolved.

We are glad we had the opportunity to book this traveling exhibit and have absolutely no regrets that we did so. It opened up our museum to folks who had never visited us before.

Sincerely,

Ken Santa
President & CEO
Castle Museum/Historical Society of Saginaw County

7

The Final Turnble Spin

Falling leaves in autumn are always a colorful reminder that February snow will soon blanket the earth. Al and I shared February birthdays although a decade apart.

It was always a moment for us to reminiscence and share our lives. As I was walking around my high school corridor listening to Motown, Al was living Motown.

Al Abrams, Motown's Gladiator Press Officer, died in the autumn of his life as his granddaughter was being born. Our Rabbi, basically, stated during Al's memorial service that one life leaves as another life is born.

Every moment in all our lives can change in one musical note.
Music, books, writing, film and politics were Al's passions. Journalism and politics aligned with his skills as an artful public relations guy.

Al won numerous journalism awards among them a Canadian award equivalent to a U.S. Pulitzer Prize. (See Michigan Rock and Roll Legends at michiganrockandroll legends.com for Al's Bio. He wrote it.)

The Detroit Motown African-American Record label is as relevant today as it puts a spin on the music that integrated America's dance floors through music. Al helped define Motown and helped propel it into becoming a mega-global record company phenomenon where skin color and world color diverged into the color of humanity.
Al, himself, was only eighteen-years-old when he immersed himself in the Black fledging record label where he coined the phrase, "Motown: The Sound of Young America".

It was devastating for Al and I when the doctor informed us that Al had two days – two weeks or two moths to live. Two weeks later, Al succumbed to cancer. But, his last two weeks of life were filled with his desire to complete his life.

He begged me to solemnly swear to fulfill the history of his life through his writing and Glass Gladiator lyrics. How does a wife deny her husband's dying request?

Al wrote two Motown manuscripts plus a few other unrelated manuscripts prior to learning of his impending death. He, also, as he was dying wrote song lyrics dedicated to gladiators who will defend humanity.

Al believed as Motown's Press Officer that the historical facts about Motown would always be revised and reinvented to serve the whims and fantasies of those who were never with Motown in 1959 helping a struggling Black record company to chart it's way with its artists to a global hit.

And, Al also believed that Motown family members would change historical fact to enhance their own biographies.

Upon Al's death, 3 October 2015, I, personally reached out to Berry Gordy for him to personalize a Motown statement about Al's death. Instead, my email was answered by Brenda Boyce. She informed me that Berry did not want to make a personalized statement, but Motown would be releasing a brief statement from Berry. She, also, instructed me that for further contact to use her AOL email. Why?

I really don't know if Berry ever received or knew about any of my emails sent to him. A statement was released by Motown on behalf of Berry. As I stated, it was brief and not what I would have expected from Berry.

Al's death was reported in almost every major global newspaper and magazine from the New York Times both online and its print edition to the Detroit Free Press to Rolling Stone Magazine Plus many more. It was, truly, amazing.

Al had always told me that he hoped he would die on a slow or no news day. He got his wish.

Al died on Saturday, 3 October 2015, as I was holding his hand. I had to have his body transported to Michigan and make all of the funeral arrangements.

Sadness surrounded me on that Fall morning. I was silently alone and lost in grief.

Al's memorial service was beautiful. It was held at The Dorfman Chapel, Farmington, Michigan. Rabbi Harold Loss officiated.

Among those who spoke at Al's service was Miss Martha Reeves. Martha also sang a few spirituals. It was heart warming.

Later I was told a story by a journalist who attended the service. Martha and he walked into the chapel together. Martha told him that she had never been a speaker at a Jewish Service and if he knew what she should say. He told Martha that he was Irish-Catholic so he didn't have a clue and told her she would be fine.

The day after Al's memorial service, I donned one of Al's shirts and sat in his favorite chair in the morning. Sipping a cup of coffee, I found the house noticeably quiet. I was deeply saddened and reflective.

Al and I always started our day with conversation. That day, I found myself talking to a purring cat.
My words are simplistic. I don't have the natural ability to write a beautiful storyline about a life that was both gracious and giving to a fault.

Al was more than simply my husband. Al became my best friend and confidante. Did we disagree and argue? Yes. Politics - People - Religious Views - Parenting - Social Media - World Issues - Animal Rights and even Movies and Music. But, we always agreed to respect our disagreements.

It was morning coffee for one. Al's matching cup was on the kitchen counter. Our morning and evening conversations had abruptly ended.

Al was the prolific writer in our family. He could take the most benign story and turn it into an intriguing and moving masterpiece of words. He believed that stories needed to reflect the individual or a story that needed to be told.

A long serving African-American judge loved Al's profile of him so much that he actually contacted him to write his obituary minus his funeral arrangements.

Al was a gentle spirit and kind soul. To him, Diversity and Humanity were one and the same. And he lived by that statement.

He loved his family, animals and the universe. His cat, Misty, was his constant companion especially when he was writing. Maybe, it was because she was not a critic.

Al was Detroit born and raised. His heart will always live on in Detroit. His soul is with God. The original Motown alumni are a close knit family but Motown needs to meld its music history and not change it.

And Al's PR work continues as his archives are extensive. Al was always proud that he was the young "persistent" Jewish teen that took Motown through racist media and PR barriers without ever realizing his own personal risks.

He had a world view where compassion and humanity had no borderlines.

He will always be Motown's original PR Gladiator Go-To-Guy. His life has become his legacy.

Memories fade --- but, legends never die as their lives become inspirational for others.

Oftentimes, I imagine that by wearing one of Al's shirts that it might somehow make me as prolific a writer as he was.

However, I do carry on conversations with Chatul, my chatty cat. Al's cat, Misty also passed away.

The Detroit sky is filled with stars representing those Motown family members who have also passed. My prayers and blessings are sent to their families.

During this unprecedented global time where the fragility of Humanity is endangering our universe, may we all find a beautiful moments to reflect as to how each of us can change the course of Humanity.

Remembering a DETROIT BOY who believed that world history could be told through generational global music.

We all have our own music play lists. Music brings us our memories, both happy and sad.

Choose a Motown record. Put the vinyl on the stereo or play on Alexa. And remember ... when.

May G-D Bless our Universe and play the music that will help us heal Humanity.

Let your LIFE MUSIC play. Let it tell your personal story.

On behalf of Al and I, please celebrate life by taking time to celebrate your own life and those you love.

May G-D Bless and Save our Universe through the heroism of Gladiators and the Diversity of Music.

Al Abrams ... Final Turntable Spin as a Glass Gladiator.

 *In Memory of*

ALAN ABRAMS
English Name

Avrum Ben Hershel
Hebrew Name

Hershel
Father's Hebrew Name

BORN
February 19, 1941
Date

DETROIT, MICHIGAN
Place of Birth

DIED
October 3, 2015
English Date of Death

20th of Tishri: 5776
Hebrew Corresponding Date

RESIDENCE
Place of Death

74
Age at Death

Statement on passing of AL ABRAMS

I am saddened to hear of the passing of Al Abrams, who was with Motown at the beginning. He was our first publicist, handling press releases and promotions. Al was smart, clever and relentless in exposing Motown to the public.

My condolences go out to his wife and family. Al will always be a part of the Motown family.

Berry Gordy,
Founder of Motown
October 5, 2015

Your Music Still Plays

For Al Abrams
& To All Those Who Made The Detroit Sound A Universal Hitsville!!!
& Especially For Barry Gordy and Michael Jackson
& For My Father, William Kingston (Al's friend) Who Played Motown All The Time.

Motown Music, all their artists and Al Abrams will be remembered forever, because music itself never gets old and a great song endures beyond the years of its artist and all the people who contributed to getting that sound to the masses. In the world of music there are many, many music companies and many, many artists, but there will only be one Motown and the people who contributed to its success. Motown, a company so unique that it needed an adjective just to describe it, The Detroit Sound!!! So here's to Hitsville USA, for the songs, for the memories, for shaping a sound that still plays today and most certainly will continue to inspire those who groove to Motown's legendary sounds, as they create the songs of tomorrow, Your Music Still Plays!!!

Your Music Still Plays
(The Song) For Al Abrams & Motown

Time spins like a record and life plays its song
We dance in a melody and sing in our song
We band together and then groups go separate ways
Knowing
A song may come to its end but the music still plays

Yes,
The chords of our lives strum many a sound
Some play rock and roll rhythm others sing like Motown
But whatever the tune that our lives dance to and play
Remember,
Every song ends but the music continues to play

For the song of each life places notes in the heart
In every person we meet who adds a chorus or part...
To the song of the Soul that shines Supreme everyday
And sings out
Your song may seem to have ended but your light continues to play

So Al,
You're now part of the rhythm and part of the rhyme
Promoting G-d's compositions, like star songs in the sky
Cause the music you promoted, that Detroit Sound from old days
Echoes forever through the sun and the rain
Singing,
A song may have ended but the music still plays
The song may have ended but the music still plays

So never forget, music doesn't just belong to a particular era or even artists. Music belongs to all those who listen to it, create new memories from it and continue to rock it and love it. So thanks for the hits, Hitsville USA, from those who continue to listen and from those who will surely listen to your Detroit Sound tomorrow!!!

And As Al Abrams Would Want,
Let The Music Play On!!!

Eric Sander Kingston
www.ericsanderkingston.com

ACKNOWLEDGEMENTS

Al felt that his book needed to acknowledge those individuals, pets and outdoor animals that contribute to our lives. Acknowledging those that surround you
who help you through life moments should never be relegated to only those who are famous. Therefore, these acknowledgements represent Al's request for his book to be inclusive and not exclusive and celebrate those who entered our lives and made a difference.

Mildred & Harry Abrams
Hedwig & Robert Stack
Luca Eliannah Cecilia Hutka
John Christopher Hutka
Louise Hutka
Margot Emery Reiter
Ian Reiter
Deborah Reiter
Alannah Abrams
Sherrie Rae & Beav Parker
Bea Fogelman
Haley Roback, River Hutka
Cats - Chatul & Misty & BC
Dog - Winnie Brooks
Notre Dame Irish Rose (ND)
Howard Hertz, Hertz Schram
Feral Cat – Toby
Horses - Emmy & Toby
Billy Kingston
Eric Kingston
Sanford Freed
Rabbi Harold Loss, Temple Israel (Michigan)
Debbie Lantz
John & Grace Daulton Lantz
Mark & Sherry Miller
Brandon & Sonya Daniels
Jena & Sean, Laurel, Cohen Meloy

Bobbie & Alex Gingolowski
Nancy & Craig Kruse
Mark & Laura Clague
Dylan Morris
Tony Mantor
Frank Johnson
Motown Family
Miss Martha Reeves
Mary Wilson
LaMont & Cheryl (Ruffin) Robinson
Ann & Wayne Risser
Anne & Ned Pahl
Laszlo Regos
Sharninghouse Family, North Baltimore, Ohio
Joe & Casey Klein
Mike & Kari Holman
Reginald Routson
James Markham Hall, Jr.
Paul Riser, Sr.
Paul Riser, Jr.
Stephanie Campbell
Amy Carles
Joe, Chere, 'Lil' Joe Lamb
Kim Williams
Logan Williams
Dave Morrow
Courtney Rhodes – Marta Witten
Denise Zanni
Legal Aid of Western Ohio, Inc.
Terry Ahls
Dana & Deborah Aaron
Adam Worthy
Bernard Kurz
Brian McCollum
Dennis Green
Paul Bauer
Sharon Davis
David Dalton
Ray Ellis UK

Bobbie Wilson
Suzi Quatro
Mordecai (Mort) Persky (Detroit Free Press)
Jon & Lafelice Perkowski
Zach Baker
Gary Johnson
Michael Gormley
Phil Sugden & Carole Eichert
Tom & Maria Ross
Neil Rushton UK
Bill Baker UK
Glenn Gunton UK
Teddie Dalton
Beech Avenue – Findlay, Ohio
5TH Street – Findlay, Ohio
Hancock County International Women's Club, Findlay, Ohio
Gateway Church – KidsWay, Findlay, Ohio
Detroit Music Awards
MusiCares
University of Michigan Music Department
Bentley Library – University of Michigan
Windsor Star
Detroit Jewish News
State of Ohio Senior Citizen Wall of Fame
Fifth Third Bank, MCPA Wall of Fame
National Rhythm & Blues Hall of Fame
Michigan Rock and Roll Hall of Fame
Detroit Historical Museum, Detroit, MI
Stax Museum, Memphis, TN
Ali Center, Louisville, Kentucky

SPECIAL ACKNOWLEDGEMENT

Cynthia & Craig Brooks (Winnie) - You three have become my Family. After Al's untimely death, I was alone and coping with endless grief. Grief holds us hostage.

You have helped me through my personal grief with your kindness, your caring, compassion and love. Your support has and is enabling me to reflect and grow older knowing that you will always be here for me. Winnie (Your Dog) and Chatul (My Cat) have transitioned into best friends. Al would be ecstatic to know that your dog and our cat have found friendship in a world where differences often leads to global conflict.
I, also, think they both like music.

And, it is a blessing for both Al's granddaughters to be accepted and loved by you. You are the Grammy and Grandpa willing to meld your own lives into their lives.

The music book you are reading is among one of Al's last requests. He was a historian and wanted it to be published to dispel rumors and rewritten history.

May G-D bless and keep my FAMILY safe and may the MUSIC never end.

My FAMILY – Cynthia-Craig-Winnie – Luca – Margot and Chatul supported me in completing this for Al.

May G-D bless and keep my FAMILY safe and May the MUSIC never end.

G-D Bless Humanity, Generational Music and our Global Family!

www.ingramcontent.com/pod-product-compliance
Lightning Source LLC
Chambersburg PA
CBHW040251170426
43191CB00018B/2372